LIVING WITH CHINA

LIVING *with* CHINA

A MIDDLE POWER FINDS ITS WAY

WENDY DOBSON

UNIVERSITY OF TORONTO PRESS
Toronto Buffalo London

ISBN 978-1-4875-0482-3

♾ Printed on acid-free, 100% post-consumer recycled paper
with vegetable-based inks.

Library and Archives Canada Cataloguing in Publication

Title: Living with China : a middle power finds its way / Wendy Dobson.
Names: Dobson, Wendy, author.
Description: Includes bibliographical references and index.
Identifiers: Canadiana 2019011245X | ISBN 9781487504823 (hardcover)
Subjects: LCSH: China – Economic policy – 2000– | LCSH: Canada –
    Foreign economic relations – China. | LCSH: China – Foreign economic
    relations – Canada.
Classification: LCC HC427.95 .D63 2019 | DDC 338.951—dc23

University of Toronto Press acknowledges the financial assistance to its
publishing program of the Canada Council for the Arts and the Ontario Arts
Council, an agency of the Government of Ontario.

Canada Council   Conseil des Arts
for the Arts   du Canada

ONTARIO ARTS COUNCIL
CONSEIL DES ARTS DE L'ONTARIO

an Ontario government agency
un organisme du gouvernement de l'Ontario

Funded by the   Financé par le
Government   gouvernement
of Canada   du Canada

Canadä

MIX
Paper from
responsible sources
FSC® C016245

Contents

PREFACE

Canada is caught between two giant trading partners whose relationship has deteriorated as Americans challenge China's development model of state capitalism and managed markets that puts Chinese enterprises first, at home and abroad. Canada, however, long used to a unipolar world dominated by the United States, lacks a China strategy. A foundation was laid in 2016 when Prime Minister Trudeau and Premier Li Keqiang agreed to a lengthy agenda for cooperation, including a possible free trade agreement. But in less than two years, the relationship between Canada and China plunged into a deep freeze when Meng Wanzhou, chief financial officer of Huawei Technologies, China's huge, privately owned telecommunications conglomerate, arrived in Canada and the United States unexpectedly exercised a bilateral treaty to request her extradition to face criminal charges of banking and wire fraud, among others. Chinese leaders chose to blame Canada for her arrest.

These events reflect the shifting centre of gravity in the global economy, foreshadowed in my 2009 study, *Gravity Shift: How Asia's New Economic Powerhouses Will Shape the 21st Century*, which anticipated the expanded economic significance of China and India by 2030. Today, just ten years later, the post–Second World War, Western-dominated world order is evolving into one with multiple players, each with its own system of governance, but also experiencing rising living standards and rapid technological change. Americans' belief in their own primacy is increasingly out of step with this shift of gravity.

China's relationship with the United States, meanwhile, has grown into a deep economic interdependence that is particularly valued by Chinese leaders who seek a stable international environment in which to pursue the country's domestic development and continued rise. Americans, however, have come to regard China as a revisionist state, and as a strategic rival and security threat. Headlines focus on the hundreds of billions of dollars of US tariffs imposed on Chinese imports, but Americans are increasingly critical of China's management of domestic markets and President Xi Jinping's robust support for advancing China's technological supremacy, not least through his Made in China 2025 strategy.

Canada's own changing relationship with China is reflected in the transformation of the world economy. As a middle power, its diplomatic relations have stressed engagement and accommodation with China, but living with China has meant being pulled into the orbit of the deteriorating relationship between China and the United States. Pierre Elliott Trudeau once characterized Canada's relationship with the United States as like a mouse living next to an elephant, but life with two restive elephants is far more complex. Canada's ties with China are at their worst since the events of Tiananmen Square in 1989. Meanwhile Canada is caught in the escalating China-US feud over the Meng affair and, with the other members of the so-called Five Eyes intelligence partners, faces increased US pressure to ban Huawei from supplying equipment to 5G mobile wireless networks in North America and Europe.

Views differ on how to mend the rift and how long this might take. What is clear, however, is that Canada needs a comprehensive strategy for living with China. Canada can hedge its Asian bets by further developing other options – with Japan, the ten members of the Comprehensive and Progressive Agreement for Trans-Pacific

Partnership, and the Association of Southeast Asian Nations – but at the centre of any comprehensive strategy must lie China. Canadians must come to understand Chinese history, values, and institutions and their significance for the Chinese president's strategies, long and short term, at home and abroad. What is the context for Xi's energetic international economic policies and institutional proposals? What are the rationales for his politicization of markets and increasingly autocratic ways at home? These are topics in the first part of this book. The second part focuses on the context for Canada's China strategy. Here I argue that the emphasis on negotiating a free trade agreement is not a strategy, and might be the wrong goal. A better understanding of China's history and views should convince Canadians of the need for a multipronged strategy that includes trade, investment, security, and engagement with multilateral partners and the public – a strategy based on mutual respect, accommodation, and genuine discussion of differences in values and institutions.

A dynamic train of events will play out as Canadians prepare for national elections in October 2019. Key economic and technological issues likely will be on the agenda for debate, including those related to the US-China relationship, given the tidal wave of recent books on the subject. My own contribution, *Partners and Rivals: The Uneasy Future to China's Relationship with the United States*, published in 2013, examined their potential global roles in the next half-century, and predicted that neither would be able to dominate the other. This study, *Living with China*, takes the perspective of a middle power's evolving relationship with a fast-changing China, and aims to deepen Canadians' understanding of the issues and options, recognizing that any strategy Canada chooses will reflect its deep integration with the United States.

LIVING WITH CHINA

INTRODUCTION

Forty years of domestic reform and opening up to international trade and investment have modernized the Chinese economy. Today it is a commonplace to describe China in terms of its market size: as a first mover in e-commerce, the world's largest goods exporter, the largest car market, and the world's leading consumer of energy and emitter of carbon. On 3 January 2019, China's *Chang'e* IV spacecraft became the first to land on the dark side of the moon. By 2030 China's middle class is projected to exceed a billion people, and its economy to be the world's largest, overtaking that of the United States in nominal terms. Since Xi Jinping became leader of the Communist Party of China (CPC) in 2012, his policy focus has been a future-oriented long game to realize the dream of a transformed China: to become a technology leader and fully developed economy and global power by 2050.

Living with this transformed China will require an understanding of Chinese values and institutions and the leadership's goals, both long and short term. Some of these are very different than those Canada espouses. Is there sufficient goodwill and mutual respect between the two countries to accommodate differences? For decades Western leaders, including Canada's, accepted China's planned economy as a phase in its development. They assumed that, with economic modernization, income growth, and integration into the world economy, China would become more like us, adopting Western liberal values and institutions and encouraging openness and democratization. Yet leadership changes and policy directions unveiled at the 19th National Congress of the CPC in November 2017 made it clear that China was on its own path, with its own development model of authoritarian state capitalism and managed markets, which continues to attract popular support among the Chinese people as long as it delivers economic growth.

Canada thus will have to learn to live with China on its own terms. Part of that learning, and a major theme of this book, is about President Xi Jinping's emphasis on maintaining political stability by consolidating his power and inserting Party control more deeply into China's economic life, even at the expense of other priorities of growth and employment, innovation, and modernizing the financial system. Part of that learning also involves Xi's ambitious goals for China: to lead a new global order as it gains prominence in diplomacy, manufacturing, technology, and transcontinental connectivity in the Belt and Road Initiative.

As Xi proudly extols China's development model and his global goals to domestic audiences, these projects and ambitions raise tensions with the West. In the United States, the Trump administration is an increasingly vocal critic of China's push to dominate future technologies, and has complained of China's failure to reciprocate its firms' access to Western markets. Market distortions created by subsidies to targeted industries and state-owned enterprises (SOEs) are of specific concern, as are unfair business practices requiring foreign investors to form joint ventures, agree to forced technology transfers, and satisfy local-content requirements. According to estimates by the Organisation for Economic Co-operation and Development (OECD), China has the highest barriers to foreign direct investment (FDI) of any major economy. In early 2019, however, heeding the Trump administration's sharp criticisms and fearing the risk of more punitive US tariffs and a costly and self-defeating trade war, China decided to liberalize its FDI policies, although the ambitious state role in advanced technologies remains.

China's goals for its domestic economic strategy are evolving. The country's economic reform was achieved largely by becoming the "workshop of the world," based on investments in export-oriented goods production and taking advantage of foreigners' interest in China's plentiful low-cost labour. After four decades of "growth at any cost," however, China's growing middle class is now expressing increasing concerns about rising income and wealth inequality and the environmental costs of rapid growth. In 2007 former premier Wen Jiabao declared that the development model, so heavily reliant on exporting industrial production, had run its course and was "unsustainable, uncoordinated, unbalanced and unstable." By the time Xi Jinping became leader, the Party had begun to respond to popular demands to realize more social and material gains. In 2017, at the 19th Party Congress, Xi announced a commitment to rebalancing domestic economic goals: "what we now face is the contradiction between unbalanced and inadequate development and the people's ever-growing needs for a better life." Resolving this contradiction involves downgrading official quantitative growth targets – even allowing slower growth. It implies replacing targets used for performance evaluations of officials at all levels with qualitative indicators. It also requires relying less on industrial growth and more on services-based, consumer-oriented growth, and less on simply adding more labour and capital, to increase output and more on innovation and technology. Official inspection tours in April 2019 emphasized anti-poverty programs and a new pro-business agenda.

This official shift of focus to an outward looking China with more centralized power has also attracted attention abroad and pushback at home. Xi's strong state leadership emphasizes a reformed military and an attack on corruption, both seen as essential to consolidating the power to purify the Party of the dishonesty and cronyism that had become prevalent as the lines between Party and business blurred during the boom years of the 1990s.

But redrawing the line has sent mixed signals. Party cells became obligatory in the governance and strategies of both state-owned and private enterprises. Powerful interests were also affected, so the anti-corruption campaign helped to silence opponents, but with unintended outcomes. Many members of the legal community were alienated, and interest group leaders and officials were intimidated and increasingly reluctant to risk innovating or adopting new ideas. The Party now faces a profound political question: Can an unrepresentative, autocratic Party be sufficiently responsive to an increasingly demanding middle class?

Xi's development model faces other challenges as well. Initiatives to promote "growth at any cost" relied on readily available state financing, which increased the indebtedness of businesses and local governments. Western analysts and foreign investors now voice serious concerns about the risks of widespread default and financial meltdown. They regard China's economic growth, based on its unprecedented success in mobilizing capital and a vast supply of low-cost labour, as vulnerable to challenge by other fast-growing, low-income countries. China's productivity growth and efficiency increases are a growing concern as Xi becomes increasingly statist, valuing political stability above all, willing to trade off efficiency to win the assent of powerful interest groups, and addressing concerns about labour layoffs by delaying the closure of aging, unproductive "zombie" factories. In short, the state as owner, producer, and regulator is ready and willing to delay economic reforms, however much they might be needed, if they pose a risk for political stability.

The Party faces a delicate balancing act between retaining its legitimacy and exercising its power to serve both the national interest and the interests of powerful groups and factions. At the end of Xi Jinping's first term in 2018, the established two-term limit for the president was abolished, setting off an intense debate about the consequences. Widespread criticism depicted the rule change as personalized, self-serving, and a bid to monopolize power that rejected Deng Xiaoping's collective leadership model of deal making and compromise. Even those who accepted it as necessary to consolidate leaders' power in order to push ahead with key reforms considered it a bad decision. Since regional interests also play a key role in the balance of power, Xi's regional experience might have been a contributing factor. Clues about his real intentions could be revealed in late 2019 at a scheduled meeting of the CPC Central Committee.

I return to these international and domestic dimensions of the long game in subsequent chapters. In Chapter 1, I focus on three challenges Xi and the Party face in "getting the economic house in order." Addressing these challenges will require managing the tension between state intervention and market reform that figured so prominently in earlier Party deliberations. The first challenge is to maintain economic growth that is strong enough to avoid the political risks of a slowdown. Here, Xi's clear preference for relying on the state as the engine of growth has starved the private sector of capital, forcing the authorities to impose lending quotas on state-owned banks. The second challenge is to modernize and open up China's financial system. The status quo primarily serves the state, as in the days of the closed economy and central planning. A modernized system would feature the internationalization of China's currency, the renminbi, allowing it to be widely used in global markets, with regulators and the central bank allowing market forces greater freedom. The third challenge is to address the low productivity of SOEs by reducing the politicization of economic decision making. Following implosions in equity and financial markets in 2015 and 2016, the slow pace of reform increased concerns about the Party's declining commitment to market forces. Capital controls reduced outward investment, while deleveraging reduced private enterprises' access to low-cost financing from shadow banks and gave SOEs, through their ready access to state financing, a new lease on life.

In Chapter 2 the focus shifts to innovation and productivity growth, which both Chinese and Americans agree are key to long-term sustainable growth. China has had some outstanding innovation successes in privately owned e-commerce enterprises. But it is the state that leads the ambitious "Made in China 2025" (MIC 2025) industrial strategy to push the country's industry up global value chains in advanced manufacturing – and the state intends to do this with generous subsidies, top-down regulations, restricted entry of foreign producers, and unfair business practices. Exploring these strategies, I find evidence of the adaptation of existing technologies, rather than the creation of new ones. These adaptations respond to Chinese conditions of market size, speed of imitation, intense competition, and official support for innovation. There is also evidence of lesser-known, but significant and uniquely Chinese, changes in industrial processes in research and development (R&D) and innovation that effectively are accelerating economic change and increasing efficiency in a number of industries. The state's willingness to protect innovators and producers from foreign competition by restricting entry is a contributing factor for the success of other enterprises. From China's perspective, the dynamism of e-commerce and the successful adaptation of existing technologies suggest that these protectionist practices have served its short-term interests.

In Chapter 3, I examine China's evolving financial system. The internationalization of the renminbi would be seen as emblematic of a great trading nation, but achieving this objective faces familiar tensions between state and market. Carefully sequenced market-based reforms will be required to create a financial system that is resilient in the face of market volatility while maintaining economic and political stability. To participate fully in the market-based global financial system, China will have to reduce restrictions on cross-border capital flows. The authorities will have to step back from overall control of the financial system, and concentrate instead on managing the risks to the currency of increased volatility due to greater exposure to external shocks to interest rates and economic demand.

The goal of internationalization adds urgency to the need to increase the transparency of China's developing bond and equity markets, to introduce market-determined prices, and to reduce state ownership of banks. Indeed these priorities have superseded internationalization, as high levels of corporate and local government indebtedness have raised the possibility of default and a "hard landing." Although recent reforms have rendered such an outcome less likely, state-owned commercial banks dominate the financial sector and are the main recourse for heavily indebted corporate borrowers, mainly SOEs, and local governments. In 2017 Xi warned that financial risk was a national security threat. Has he mobilized an adequate response? Are recent reforms – the restructuring of financial regulation, increased oversight by both the State Council and the central bank, and the creation of a high-level Financial Stability and Development Commission chaired by a vice premier – adequate to support China's long game?

I turn to this long game in Chapters 4 and 5. Closely linked to China's innovation and financial policies are its "going out" policies, which encourage both cooperation with and acquisition of foreign firms to acquire new assets and technologies. In Chapter 4 I examine China's outward direct investment performance over the 2013–17 period as investments in North America and Europe surged before slowing markedly in 2017, when regulatory restrictions were tightened. A comparison of the top ten deals in 2016 and 2017 illustrates the tensions between market forces and state intervention in both sending and host countries. For example, although acquisitions of US firms dominated Chinese firms' top ten deals in 2016, no US firms appeared on the 2017 list. A key driver of these foreign acquisitions was China's slowing growth rate, which sent many investors abroad to seek higher-growth opportunities, while others sought to escape regulatory restrictions within China. The scale of these capital outflows and their negative effects on the exchange rate led to an official crackdown in 2017. Given the interventions by regulatory authorities and the central bank since then, what can one expect of China as a global investor in the years ahead? One clue was offered at the 2019 World Economic Forum in Davos, Switzerland, when the chair of Sinochem, one of China's largest chemical groups, predicted that overseas investment by Chinese companies would slow at least until trade tensions eased with the United States.

The subject of Chapter 5 is the Belt and Road Initiative (BRI), a visionary but controversial infrastructure investment project intended to connect China, its Asian neighbours, and European and African economies. The BRI has been described variously as a twenty-first-century version of the fabled Silk Road and as China's project of the century. These are early days, but already there is evidence that physical infrastructure and renminbi-based trading are helping to create new opportunities for the estimated seventy countries participating in the BRI, many on the periphery, that collectively account for 62 per cent of the world's population and more than 30 per cent of global gross domestic product (GDP).

At the project level, however, the BRI has sent mixed signals in its initial five years. Many projects were structured to serve Chinese employment and business objectives, rather than assisting the development of local economies. Projects in a lengthening list of countries, including Pakistan and Sri Lanka, have drawn strong criticisms of China for practising "debt trap diplomacy," whereby Chinese banks make loans that a country is unable to repay, forcing the debtor to use the assets from a project as repayment and effectively transferring local assets to Chinese owners. I review these and other lessons of the BRI's first five years in Chapter 5, and note China's new willingness to collaborate with multilateral partners such as the World Bank and the International Monetary Fund (IMF), which have long experience with funding large infrastructure projects. Of central importance are the design and preparation of investments to ensure they are "debt sustainable" – that debts incurred are of a size the borrower can repay without "debt distress" that requires debt reduction or restructuring.

Canada is the focus of Chapter 6. As a middle power accustomed to a unipolar world dominated by the United States, the implications for Canada of China's international emergence are sobering. In particular, Canada will have to find its way in the increasingly complex relationship between China and the United States, its two largest trading partners.

China's economic environment sends mixed signals about the relationship between the state and markets. Although Xi Jinping accords preference to relatively unproductive SOEs, other industries, such as e-commerce, make up a dynamic and highly competitive private sector that has to find ways to co-exist with SOEs, such as partnering with them and accepting Party cells to monitor social responsibility. The US critique of this increasing role of the state, of Chinese antipathy towards foreign entrants, and of their resort to unfair business practices are important sources of tensions in the US-China trade relationship.

As China becomes a global investor, it is increasing its leadership profile in international institutions. It is also pursuing cross-border initiatives, creating its own international development institutions, such as the Asian Infrastructure Investment Bank, and spearheading ambitious technological and international initiatives with MIC 2025 and the BRI. Can such initiatives sustain both competition *and* the cooperation necessary to maintain global peace and prosperity? The current US administration thinks the answer is "no," for reasons relating to another theme in this book: Xi Jinping's growing aspirations for China's global influence and leadership in advanced technologies. Will China and the United States evolve towards geopolitical parity, or will China seek regional or global dominance? The United States' definition of China as a strategic rival and revisionist power leaves little doubt about growing US mistrust, effectively abandoning a long-established policy of constructive engagement and deeper interdependence.

Canada's interests unequivocally lie in peaceful partnerships and mutual accommodation. But the US extradition request for Huawei chief financial officer Meng Wanzhou and her subsequent arrest in Vancouver in December 2018 added a new dimension of complexity among the three governments, plunging the Canada-China relationship into a diplomatic deep freeze amid charges by Chinese officials that Canada was merely placating the United States. Canada will have to manage the relationship with China according to its own values and in pursuit of the the goal of reducing dependence on the US market. But Canada also must honour long-standing legal agreements with its US neighbour that make it difficult to bridge differences in Canadian and Chinese values and institutions and build mutual trust with China.

In Chapter 6, I propose elements of a China strategy that uses the relationship prior to the recent diplomatic deep freeze as the baseline. Canadians have been slow to learn about modern China and to accept that it is not, and will not be, "like us." I argue that Canada's strategic agenda should serve its long-term economic and security objectives. The agenda should recognize differences and seek to manage them, guided by leadership from the top. The narrative for deeper engagement should recognize not only Canada's interest in diversifying its trade, but also China's importance to Canada's goal of a peaceful and cooperative world order.

In this broader context, I explore the possibilities for and ways to liberalize Canada's trade and investment ties with China. I argue that the *sine qua non* is not necessarily a formal bilateral free trade agreement, which has been the subject of much political rhetoric and the focus of US criticism in the new US-Mexico-Canada Agreement (USMCA). Alternatives to free trade, such as sectoral initiatives and bilateral and multilateral economic partnership agreements, are widely used in Asia. Canada's bilateral trade with China is largely complementary: Canada produces an abundance of natural resources, energy, and food, while China seeks security of supply. A new China strategy should also take into account Canada's national security and defence priorities and its participation in East Asia's regional security institutions. Beyond negotiations on traditional tariffs, quotas, and services, other trade-related issues should be addressed to bridge differences in institutions, laws, and standards, and policies developed towards cyber security, intellectual property (IP) protection, and privacy issues associated with digitalization and artificial intelligence.

Also part of this broader context are soft-power issues such as China's treatment of its Uighur minority, the bad press generated by poorly planned BRI projects, actions against Canadians in China in retaliation for Meng's arrest in Vancouver, and China's rejection of Canada's proposed gender, labour standards, and environmental issues on its progressive trade agenda. China's use of the diaspora to influence policies and attitudes towards China has also contributed to a backlash in Canada. Rather than relying on bilateral modes of engagement, working with coalitions and allies might be a more effective approach for Canada.

The picture of Canada's life with China is a dynamic and uncertain one. In the short term, decisions by Canadian courts will determine the prospects for continued engagement. Can the relationship be normalized if judicial proceedings in Canada reject the US extradition request for Meng even as other criminal charges play out in US courts? Will a ruling that permits Meng's extradition continue the diplomatic deep freeze or worsen it? Whatever happens,

Canada will need to continue to find a way to live with China by carrying through its commitment to promote trade, investment, security, and other common interests, seeking to engage Communist Party officials and civil society in the pursuit of global and long-term interests, while standing up for its values.

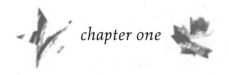

chapter one

CHINA'S RISE:
GETTING ITS HOUSE IN ORDER

China's rise and economic transformation have been driven by favourable demographics, a high saving rate, and impressive industrial investment by both Chinese and foreigners as the country opened up to the world. But China's progress has not been without its problems and related challenges of managing the tensions of a politicized market place and growing statism under President Xi Jinping.

Even as China becomes more of a global force, its leaders are preoccupied with "getting its house in order" with reforms that address risks while serving the Party's primary goal of political stability. Three priorities stand out: maintaining economic growth at sustainable rates, dealing with the systemic risks posed by an immature financial system as China becomes a global player, and addressing the persistent low productivity of state-owned enterprises. The existing development model encouraged massive rural-urban migration, raised incomes, and supported the emergence of a burgeoning middle class, but these have come at a heavy cost. The polluted environment endangers people's health; incomes and wealth are unequally distributed;[1] the some 150,000 SOEs have supported industrial growth rates by borrowing to finance their activities and running up large debts that outstrip their ability to repay.

As the Party responds to the contradiction between pursuing "growth at any cost" and popular demands for a better quality of life, economic growth must also satisfy the implicit social contract between the people and the Party whereby the people tolerate the Party's autocratic ways in exchange for steady improvements in jobs and living standards. It is to these ends that China is restructuring and rebalancing its low-cost, labour-intensive, export-oriented industrial base to one that is more services-based, consumer-oriented, and productivity driven – and sustainable. Improving productivity performance will support slower but more sustainable growth; at the officially anticipated annual real rate of around 6 per cent, the economy would double in size every twelve years.

The reform agenda, however, is highly politicized. To restore a power base free of corruption, the Party is seeking changes affecting all major interest groups within government, the military, and the economy. To counterbalance the resulting political pressures, Xi has centralized administrative power.[2] The anti-corruption campaign is part of this evolving structure, as are a National Security Council and small leading groups that oversee various policy areas and report directly to Xi. The anti-corruption campaign is popular because of its focus on reducing the misuse of political privilege that had become widespread among Party members and elites. In March 2018 a National Supervisory Commission was inaugurated with the mandate to broaden the anti-corruption campaign beyond the Party to "all public posts."[3]

No one expects China to be problem-free with these changes. At the National People's Congress in March 2018, Xi focused on three "tough battles" in the real economy: addressing financial risks, reducing poverty, and tackling pollution. The poverty-reduction battle emphasizes poverty relief, improved market access for production from poorer regions, and access to better education and health services.[4] Modernizing the financial system and developing a greener and cleaner economy are part of rebalancing the economy to rely more on services sectors and on innovation and productivity performance to drive growth.

At the same time, Xi is pursuing his dream of a major rejuvenation to restore China's greatness in the world. Global benchmarks are apparent in vows of Chinese leadership in global forums and in initiatives to become a world military power and technology leader and to expand China's global influence through infrastructure investments and connectivity. China is engaged in potentially game-changing initiatives such as the Belt and Road Initiative, which are ambitious and risky and not yet well understood in Western countries, where there is a tendency to focus on and magnify the risks of failure.

These aspirations and the prospect of China's eclipsing the United States as the world's largest economy by 2030 or sooner (Figure 1.1) have strengthened expectations of a global shift in economic and political power. Different measures of GDP give differing crossover points. In Figure 1.1, the measure is US dollar GDP measured in current dollars, and the crossover point is estimated to be 2027, according to the International Monetary Fund. Another commonly used measure is purchasing power parity (PPP), which takes into account the cost of living in respective countries. Since Chinese prices are

Figure 1.1 Trajectory of Growth of Gross Domestic Product, China and the United States, 1980–2034

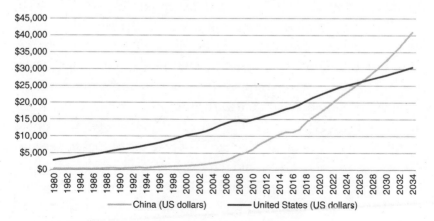

lower than US prices, a given dollar amount of income goes much further than in the United States. By PPP measures, China's GDP eclipsed that of the United States in 2014.

The outcome of the 2016 US presidential election unexpectedly added to this narrative, as the new president projected a view of each nation on its own, rather than continuing to cooperate in the post-war US-led world order. Preoccupations with "America First" and "making America great again" marked a significant shift towards zero-sum policy thinking. Together with an erratic, transactional approach to international relations, a vacuum in global leadership has opened, one that China could move to fill.

Indeed Xi Jinping aspires to shape reforms in global governance, as he made clear in a June 2018 speech, when he predicted that, by 2050, China will have become "a leader of composite national strength and international influence." Xi also called for China to "lead the reform of the global governance system with the concepts of fairness and justice," signalling what former Australian prime minister Kevin Rudd predicted is likely to be a wave of Chinese international policy activism.[5]

Xi has elaborated this theme in a series of high-profile international events since 2014. That year, China chaired the Asia-Pacific Economic Cooperation (APEC) summit, at which negotiating a Free Trade Area of the Asia-Pacific was proposed. In 2015 China and the United States also worked out a joint leadership initiative on climate change at talks leading to the Paris Agreement on Climate Change. In 2015 as well, as part of the BRI, China launched the Asian Infrastructure Investment Bank, a new multilateral institution to help fund major infrastructure and connectivity investments in the region and beyond. In 2016 China hosted the annual meeting of G20 leaders in Hangzhou, where the central theme was "building an innovative, invigorated, interconnected and inclusive world economy." In January 2017 Xi's keynote speech to the World Economic Forum in Davos, Switzerland, further committed

China to building a moderately prosperous future with a community of shared destinies for humanity and win-win cooperation. In April 2017 Xi's first official meeting with the new US president, Donald Trump, set an initial positive tone at the top in the bilateral relationship. In his April 2018 keynote speech to the Boao Forum for Asia, entitled "Openness for Greater Prosperity, Innovation for a Better Future," Xi committed to strengthened protection of IP rights and to opening up more of the Chinese economy by liberalizing trade and investment – reforms very much in line with political priorities for the bilateral relationship.[6] In a 2019 visit to Rome, Xi welcomed Italy's endorsement of the BRI, the first such commitment by a G7 government, and at the second Belt and Road Forum in Beijing in April 2019 he elaborated further on these themes.

This is a remarkable series of positive messages about how Chinese interests include commitments to the world's collective future, but Chinese and Americans interpret them very differently. China realizes it is a big beneficiary of globalization. China's economic growth – and access to foreign investment, trade, and ideas – has been spectacularly successful in pulling people out of poverty. In contrast the United States is struggling with the political fallout from an economy in which significant groups have fallen behind, immigration and foreigners are blamed, and public support for globalization is undermined.

The current US administration has expressed its views of China in its National Security Strategy and National Defense Strategy, both released in December 2017. These documents stereotype China as a revisionist power seeking regional hegemony in the Asia-Pacific region and projecting its power in Cold War fashion. Some experienced diplomats and analysts have discounted this approach as simplistic and lacking in understanding of Chinese motivations, while missing China's actual challenge. China, they argue, is seeking neither military conflict nor to overthrow the existing system. As Paul Heer, a former national intelligence officer, maintains, the true challenge is that China is competing with the United States on its own terms, challenging the US conception of its exclusive role in the world and pursuing the dream to re-establish China's status as a great power (but not global pre-eminence).[7] China is not intimidated by any attempted US trade war, but instead is engaging in tit-for-tat. None of this, it is argued, implies a zero-sum calculus by China; instead, as Xi's speeches make clear, China acknowledges interdependence. The United States should, too, because it will have to find ways to accommodate Chinese aspirations and ambitions.

Others disagree. *Course Correction*, a 2019 report by the Asia Society's Task Force on US-China Policy, sees the two countries on a collision course as the foundations of good will built up over many years erode. Many Americans see China's rise under Xi Jinping as unfairly undercutting US prosperity and security, while Chinese increasingly view the United States as a declining power. This essential relationship, the report insists, must be prevented "from running off the rails."[8]

Understanding the changing dynamics of China's relationship with the United States is essential to Canada's learning to live with China. I return to these dynamics in later chapters; here, I focus on China's domestic economic objectives and the tensions between market forces and state intervention – both the focus of much US criticism – which complicate the rebalancing and restructuring of the Chinese economy necessary to grow at a sustainable rate. These tensions are recognized in the 13th Five-Year Plan (2016–20), and were extensively discussed in 2013 at the Third Plenum of the 18th Party Congress. At that meeting, Xi stated "the focus of the restructuring of the economic system ... is to allow the market [forces] to play a 'decisive role' in the allocation of resources."[9] These words were a call for government to withdraw from its long-established practice of pricing and allocating key production inputs such as land, capital, and energy, and instead allow the operation of market forces in deregulated and competitive product markets. Instead, in 2015–16, high-level political support for market reforms evaporated as the government scrambled to address the multiple challenges of the stock market meltdown, large capital outflows, and exchange-rate depreciation. In 2017 the state increased its role in domestic enterprises as Party members participated in decision making in both SOEs and private firms. Party cells reportedly were to be established in foreign-invested joint ventures as well.[10]

Fighting corruption, revamping the military, and national security ranked higher in Party priorities than did economic reform and modernization until 2016–17, when President Xi labelled financial risks a "threat to national security" requiring regulatory and other reforms (see Chapter 3). To avoid unwanted currency depreciation, cross-border capital flows had to be curbed, despite their importance to the open economy and the internationalization of the renminbi. To support growth objectives, banks were encouraged to finance growth-supportive corporate investments while managing them in ways that would avoid rising debt defaults in a slower-growing economy. Opening the market to foreign competition also had to be managed carefully to reduce competitive pressures on SOEs. Financed by borrowing at subsidized rates from state-owned banks, SOEs were chosen to support short-term growth objectives. With private sector indebtedness reaching levels as high as 170 per cent of GDP, however, the OECD and IMF warned of default risks and bank runs associated with a hard landing. This resulted in mixed signals, suggesting that the authorities were operating with one foot on the accelerator to meet growth targets and one foot on the brake to avoid politically risky side effects.

This tension between state and market suggests that, to the Chinese authorities, "sustainable growth" is participative and re-distributive. The 13th Five-Year Plan addresses both goals. It calls for accelerated financial reform, opening financial markets, and improving competition in "national monopoly sectors," while including resources for social welfare proposals to combat poverty, improve the social insurance system, adjust pension funds, reform public hospitals, and provide health insurance for the jobless.

Following the 19th Party Congress in late 2017 and the National People's Congress in March 2018, a new team, including Xi's allies, took charge of the Politburo Standing Committee. For this seven-person Party leadership group, tackling corruption remained a political priority that outranked the importance of economic modernization and reform – despite a strong case for the growth-augmenting potential of increasing the efficiency of SOEs and other enterprise reforms.

One notable exception to this agenda was the priority given the goal of a low-carbon future. The 13th Five-Year Plan includes a number of "green" proposals that focus on low-carbon industry systems, "green" finance, new-energy vehicles, forest protection, and an online environmental monitoring system. Since the 1970s, China's heavy reliance on coal to fuel the industrial economy has been a major source of carbon emissions. Pledges since 2009 to cut carbon intensity have been expanded to cap carbon emissions and increase the sources of non-fossil fuels to 20 per cent of energy requirements by 2030, with greenhouse gas emissions expected to peak between 2025 and 2030. Measures have already been taken to limit energy consumption and to cut energy and carbon intensity. The pragmatic introduction of market-based approaches would augment these administrative measures. At the end of 2017, a carbon-trading system was announced that covers power-generation plants, and an exchange for trading emissions permits has been given the go-ahead. What is missing is a market-determined carbon price.[11]

These actions – and inactions – speak louder than words. Additional rebalancing is required, but this is constrained by conflicting political and economic objectives. Achieving the objectives of sustainable growth, a modern financial system, and more competitive

SOEs would require structural changes that, in turn, depend on a political decision to take the foot off the brake and allow the accelerator (market forces) to work.

ACHIEVING SUSTAINABLE GROWTH: AVOIDING THE "MIDDLE-INCOME TRAP"

Major structural reforms are required to the supply side of the Chinese economy to raise productivity and encourage innovations and technologies that use capital and labour more efficiently. Such a supply-side transition will not be not easy, however, and the risks to growth are real. In 2008 the World Bank's Growth Commission found that, in the post-war period, only thirteen developing countries experienced annual growth rates of at least 7 per cent for twenty-five years or longer. These countries shared certain common characteristics that included economic openness, macroeconomic stability, committed and capable government, high rates of savings and investment, and reliance on market forces to allocate resources.[12] Studies of the reasons a country's economic growth slows or stagnates have identified a variety of factors. Commonly, as abundant labour supplies are used up and wages rise, exports become uncompetitive and growth in incomes slows unless new sources of growth are tapped, most importantly by encouraging technological development to improve productivity performance. The alternative is to risk being squeezed between low-wage competitors in mature industries and innovators in industries undergoing rapid technological change, and suffering slowing growth as a consequence. In addressing the risks of falling into this "middle-income trap" of slow or stagnant growth, each country has to find its own solution. South Korea is a well-known success story, where government stepped back from its roles as owner and intervenor in the economy and instead set the framework for the private sector and introduced supporting policies to promote more advanced education and modern finance, among other goals.

China's leaders are concerned about these risks, and since 2015 have sought to sustain growth by improving manufacturing and industrial productivity. They have set ambitious technological goals for the Made in China 2025 strategic plan. As I discuss in Chapter 2, this strategic initiative is controversial, not least because of its generous government financial support, its official emphasis on producing in China goods previously sourced abroad, and its policy discrimination favouring Chinese over foreign firms.

The contrast between these political choices and what economic theory prescribes to escape the middle-income trap can be seen in the work of Peking University professor Huang Yiping.[13] Applying lessons the World Bank's Growth Commission learned from countries that avoided the trap, Huang recommends strengthening China's research and education base, providing more education for the country's 300 million migrant workers, and further liberalization and modernization of the financial system to support the risk-taking necessary to finance technological innovation and industrial upgrading. Among the key lessons to be learned from other countries, Huang notes the importance of legal and political policies to liberalize entry to protected sectors dominated by state enterprises, and the protection of property rights in order to encourage risk-taking and innovation.

FINANCIAL MODERNIZATION AND REBALANCING

Financial system reform and modernization are integral both to achieve China's economic rebalancing objectives and to avoid the middle-income trap. SOEs figure prominently in these reforms because of their close institutional linkages with state-owned banks, which view them as low-risk, government-connected borrowers.

Until recently, debt rollovers and debt-equity conversions were favoured over defaults. As the Bank for International Settlements has estimated, however, non-financial companies account for two-thirds of China's total official debt level – one of the world's highest, exceeding 260 per cent of GDP – with SOEs accounting for one of the most serious debt problems.[14]

At the July 2017 meeting of the National Financial Work Conference, Xi Jinping identified financial risks as a national security threat, and in his opening speech to the 19th Party Congress later in the year he stressed SOE indebtedness as a priority. He also underscored the need for deleveraging, which would require a shift away from the quantitative growth targets that drove borrowing in the first place. To that end, moves to strengthen the powers of China's financial regulators and improve coordination among them were a key policy outcome of the National Financial Work Conference.[15] In 2018 the IMF, in its Article IV consultation report, welcomed China's formation of a Financial Stability and Development Committee, chaired by Vice-Premier Liu He.[16] The IMF emphasized the importance of assessing the evolution of systemic risks in particular, and recommended that China strengthen its regulatory and macroprudential policy framework.[17]

The overall performance of China's financial institutions is strongly influenced by that of four large state-owned commercial banks that dominate China's financial sector and its role in supporting the real economy. The negative consequences of shadow banking activities and the ready supply of credit to connected state-owned borrowers are well known. These practices have troubled the IMF, which, after warning against them in 2016, subsequently supported measures to rein in the interbank borrowing, proliferating wealth-management products, and off-balance-sheet activities that were riskier parts of the immature financial system. Notably, the outcomes included a smaller shadow banking sector and reduced connections between banks and non-banks.[18] Following the March

2019 National People's Congress, People's Bank of China governor Yi Gang signalled further reforms to improve investors' risk management by freeing up prices in capital markets and expanding the supply of hedging tools.

One increasingly dynamic feature of China's financial sector is Internet finance, which includes deposits, loans, investments, insurance, equity crowdfunding, and Internet fund sales, and is creating alternative financial instruments and channels for consumers, savers and investors. Online consumer financial services to savers and lenders has proliferated rapidly in this environment. Initial official supervision of these Internet activities was light, as regulators practised forbearance and watched and learned as the industry evolved. But fraudulent operators took advantage of the regulatory vacuum, creating new risks that led to a crackdown by the central bank and financial regulators in 2016–17. The bank led multiple agencies in designing a cleanup plan and a crackdown on fraudulent online payments, peer-to-peer (P2P) lending, equity crowdfunding, wealth management, and online insurance. Agencies in the provinces that register corporations were instructed to reject any new registrations of companies with "finance" in their names or business descriptions.[19] The State Council set up a task force involving ten agencies to better regulate Internet finance and introduce measures to reduce risk, improve the competitive environment, and boost risk awareness of investors.[20] In May 2017 the People's Bank of China replaced its technology department with an oversight committee "to oversee financial technology" in light of the speedy growth of the industry and in recognition of cross-sector financial risks.[21] Subsequently, in July 2018, the central bank opened a third-party payment platform called Nets Union Clearing Corporation, which subjects all financial transactions of third-party-payment firms such as Alipay and TenPay to regulatory oversight. By the end of that year, the combined negative growth effects of uncertainties generated by the US-China trade dispute and the regulatory crackdown on shadow banks were evident as market forces were allowed to set prices. The benchmark Chinese Securities Index 300 ended the year down more than 25 per cent over the previous year, compared with an 8 per cent decline in the S&P 500 index. New daily mark-to-market requirements played a significant role by eliminating the perception that such prices were guaranteed.[22]

These financial reforms are key features of China's larger quest for financial modernization and rebalancing. But the timing and somewhat ad hoc implementation of regulatory reforms created problems that proved to be disruptive in mid-2018 as P2P investors, faced with the government's emphasis on deleveraging, sought to monetize their assets only to find that many borrowers had defaulted or the platform owners had run off with their money. P2P lending collapsed in mid-2018, requiring regulatory standardization throughout the industry that would take a year or more to implement.[23] Despite these problems, official support for further development of the P2P industry has continued in recognition of the scarcity of alternative credit sources for consumers and the many small businesses unable to access more conventional lenders.

SOE REFORM: THE PARTY RUNS THE ECONOMY

SOE reform is a contentious issue within China's rebalancing strategy. Under the status quo, numerous "zombie" firms are kept alive with loans from the state-owned banks, mainly to maintain employment levels regardless of borrowers' underlying competitiveness. Western economists prescribe more efficient measures, such as swapping debt for equity, encouraging firms suffering from temporary market setbacks to issue shares to management as incentive payments, or merging with more successful competitors. Uncompetitive zombies would be forced into bankruptcy. In contrast, Chinese reform objectives emphasize "bigger is better," with government retaining its ownership of the largest SOEs and re-shuffling their assets to reduce excess capacity while increasing their sectoral concentration. Private investors are meant to be attracted to specified "strategic" industries aligned with an import-substitution industrial policy. The expressed goal is to improve SOE efficiency and productivity, but the implicit goal is to do so without generating large-scale unemployment.

A long list of industries has been reserved for SOEs, including defence, state monopolies in oil and electricity, telecoms and transportation (for example, rail, aerospace, and auto producers), construction, finance, metals, and mining, although restrictions are being relaxed to permit 50 per cent private ownership on a case-by-case basis. Privately owned enterprises are dominant in manufacturing and a range of tertiary industries, including leasing and commercial services, scientific research and polytechnical services, information technology (IT), real estate, resident and other services, transport storage, and postal services, as well as, to some extent, health care and education.[24]

The planning mentality in SOE policy has a long history. Prior to the 1980s, SOEs accounted for 80 per cent of total output, a share that has since declined to around 20 per cent.[25] As many as 150,000 SOEs still exist, however – two-thirds of them owned by local governments. SOEs account for about half of the national total of bank loans and for a major share of troubled corporate debt. Reforming the state sector involves at least partial privatization of some SOEs and allowing others to go bankrupt. Those that remain are gradually being consolidated and encouraged to grow through domestic mergers and international acquisitions. Rationalization of SOEs in polluting industries such as steel and cement will be managed according to such criteria as geographic concentration and their potential employment implications. The latter, indeed, are the subject of debate, with some prominent voices arguing that additional government funding should not go to the state sector if the primary purpose is to maintain jobs in zombie firms. The funds would be better used to help laid-off workers find new jobs in the private sector – the underlying principle being to "protect people, not companies or jobs."[26]

The role of SOEs was intensely debated in 2013 at and following the Third Plenum of the 18th Party Congress, but the outcome was ambiguous. New goals assigned to SOEs reflected a mix of objectives. For example, SOEs were directed to develop new technologies and become national champions, but champions that were to maintain economic stability by investing when growth slows and by leading sectoral restructuring.[27] Finance ministry proposals to impose budget constraints and rate-of-return objectives on SOEs were ignored. Instead SOEs were chosen to drive the transition to a more innovative, advanced manufacturing economy. In effect, the short-term outcome was to increase reliance on SOEs.

Mergers and acquisitions among SOEs followed, creating huge entities. In 2015 COSCO and China Shipping merged, creating the world's fourth-largest container shipping company, and in November 2016 Wuhan Iron and Steel and Baosteel merged to form the country's largest steelmaker. The State-owned Assets Supervision and Administration Commission, which is responsible for SOEs, has pushed for more and larger national champions. To that end, it has combined the largest railway equipment makers, and is reported to have its eye on chemical producers.[28] In mid-2017 two other SOEs merged, one a very large coal-fired-power generator and the other the largest coal-mining enterprise, to create the world's largest power generator.

Private capital has also been sought to revitalize SOEs. In a high-profile transaction in mid-2017, Alibaba, Tencent, Baidu, JD.com, and Didi Chuxing rode to the rescue of China Unicom, the country's second-largest telecom SOE, with estimated investments of nearly $12 billion in new and existing shares of the company's unit listed on the Shanghai Stock Exchange; SOE capital was also included, as China Life Insurance bought a large share (all dollar amounts in this book are US dollars).[29]

In 2018 SOEs also acquired troubled privately owned enterprises whose growth had slowed with the slower-growing economy and the introduction of measures to rein in shadow banks, on which such enterprises had depended for capital. By September, SOEs had acquired ten privately owned groups, touching off a debate about the negative effects of state ownership on innovation and revitalizing the economy. It was also noted that private groups in sectors dominated by SOEs, including steel, coal, and aluminum, had suffered disproportionately from factory closures and production limits.[30]

An outstanding question about these state-related reforms is whether size will matter more than performance and efficiency. Rationalization and modernization are required at the micro level to cut subsidies, reform tax incentives, place more emphasis on quality control, and promote best practices. A 2016 IMF study of the SOE reform strategy expresses scepticism that it will improve resource allocation. By IMF estimates, an alternative reform package of debt restructuring, hard budget constraints, more competition, and the provision of financial support to workers, rather than to firms, would, along with complementary reforms, raise output between 3 and 9 per cent in the medium term.[31] This is a sober reminder of the cost of maintaining the status quo.

Some promising reform ideas are in play, such as allowing the award of share ownership to employees of SOEs in order to give them a stake in their firm's commercial success. SOEs are also being reclassified as commercial or public services, allowing the former to be treated more like private businesses. Most public attention has focused on mixed ownership reforms like those in the China Unicom deal. SOEs that sell shares to private investors, however, can expect to be subjected to more challenging demands than would be forthcoming from the state. A key problem is that potential investors would be unwilling to become co-owners of zombie or struggling firms when the state remains reluctant to give private investors more strategic influence by allowing them majority stakes.

Giving boards of directors of SOEs more say is another reform option that has not materialized; instead the Party is increasing its own control. SOEs will continue to access cheap capital, but are expected to follow the government's agenda. As noted earlier, SOEs are required to have an Enterprise Party Committee with a mandate to review major strategic decisions before they are presented to the board – with this imposition the Party, in effect, is acting as owner.[32] SOE officials are also being subjected to stepped-up political education, making them more risk averse in the wake of the anti-corruption campaign and undermining both morale and performance. As Nicholas Lardy (2019) argues, the state has "struck back": Xi Jinping has repeatedly emphasized the increasing importance of SOEs while reducing the roles of market forces and private enterprises.[33]

The drive for "national champion" SOEs has international implications. SOEs have moved into international markets in such industries as construction, steel, and railways to increase their business and participate in state-backed large infrastructure projects such as the BRI. If these national champions are seen to push other firms and bidders aside, they could provoke a public backlash against Chinese capital. Another source of potentially negative international reaction could be expected from huge "megamerger" SOEs that encounter execution difficulties – a common risk in completing mergers everywhere. Such difficulties and even failures of mergers could also create negative spillovers and backlash beyond the Chinese economy. A third concern is the appearance of state capital investment and operation companies, created to manage existing state assets and to invest in new assets, including in privately owned enterprises in the fast-growing consumer, health care, and IT sectors. Will state investors convert these more-productive private enterprises into SOEs, with consequential negative effects on efficiency and innovation? How wise will the state be as investor? Crowding out private investors could cause another backlash as investors demand state assistance in order to compete.

MORE BALANCE NEEDED FOR SUCCESSFUL ECONOMIC RESTRUCTURING

Chinese leaders' reform strategy and pursuit of great power status for China will have significant implications for the rest of us. As we have seen, restructuring the supply side of the economy requires institutional and policy reforms and innovations that raise productivity and use available capital more efficiently. Further rationalization of inefficient and loss-making SOEs is unfinished business dating back to the 1990s, and then premier Zhu Rongji's energetic campaign to withdraw intervention, permit bankruptcies, and privatize underperforming SOEs contrasts sharply with the mixed messages sent out today. Everyone has a stake in seeing China succeed, not least because of the political risks of negative spillovers should one of the world's largest economies experience a financial crisis. Even in a more benign outcome, China will choose its own mix of state and market. The Chinese economy cannot be expected to converge with the market economies of the West, and Western countries, including Canada, will have to come to grips with that reality in learning to live with China.

The recurring theme in this book is thus one of tension and balance. Restructuring or rebalancing the Chinese economy is a clear objective. Balance is also sought between the Party's political objectives for stability and freeing market forces to sustain economic growth at rates sufficient to avoid the middle-income trap. But tensions are evident. Xi Jinping has increased his autocratic control of China's institutions of power. He has increased repression and prescribed greater political content in academic curricula and the control of universities and non-governmental organizations, presumably to rein in actions or writings that might challenge the Party's legitimacy. The growth implications of this politicization of economic institutions and policy seemed to be secondary considerations. Yet, at the March 2019 National People's Congress, leaders stressed risks to economic growth and moved to improve the business environment by reducing taxes. There were other signs of change, if not of changing the game, in the declining leverage of corporate China and local governments. China's innovation performance will be a critical factor in its economic future and its influence in the world. Here again there are mixed signals from the state: encouragement to reach the technological frontier, but in state-approved ways, rather than by riskier, market-led, bottom-up innovations and protection of IP rights. Innovation is the subject to which I turn in the next chapter.

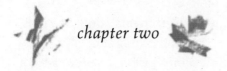

chapter two

CHINA AS A GLOBAL INNOVATOR?

In late 2017 a headline in the *South China Morning Post* declared: "China's chance to lead global innovation may lie with 5G mobile technology development."[1] The accompanying story began as follows: "China is on the cusp of recasting itself as a leading technology innovator from a mere follower in the telecommunications industry," a statement that conveys China's growing ambitions to create new technologies, rather than adapt existing ones.[2] These ambitions are rooted in China's history, as westerners were reminded by the elaborate opening ceremonies at the 2008 Beijing Summer Olympics. Troops of performers colourfully celebrated China's historical record as the inventor of gunpowder, the compass, paper, and moveable type, while its use of hydraulics and iron smelting predated such knowledge in Europe.

Since 2006 China has been in fast-forward mode as government ministries have rolled out successive ambitious plans to make the country an innovative society, with growing emphasis on science and technology and the declared aim to become a world leader in advanced manufacturing and, more recently, artificial intelligence (AI). Innovation performance is a central factor – as part of broader structural changes – in achieving more sustainable growth after decades of investment-led, export-oriented, rapid industrial growth. Initially that industrial growth was driven simply by adding more capital and labour, redeploying China's abundant supplies of rural, low-cost labour to modern urban jobs, and encouraging the investment of domestic and foreign capital. As the labour force became more productive, wages rose, as did consumption. But China's population is aging as a result of the one-child policy and the labour force has begun to shrink, reducing growth prospects, increasing uncertainty about investment projects, and reducing investment efficiency. Where, for decades, China had used three to four units of capital to produce an additional unit of output, in the 2010–15 period 5.6 units were required.[3] Improving productivity growth through innovation became a priority.

CHINESE INNOVATION STRATEGIES

Innovation takes a variety of forms and produces a variety of outcomes. The goal of innovation is to create new knowledge and apply it in commercial applications to attain economic advantage. The innovation process involves learning by entrepreneurs and creative thinkers who design new ways of doing things; firms devise strategies, solve problems, and find new ways to deliver more output per unit of input, often through risky processes of trial and error. Innovation includes activities that range from discovery and invention to the adaptation and incremental upgrading of existing products, processes, and practices.

Much Chinese innovation, however, has been characterized as adaptation or "incrementally upgraded products with unprecedented rapidity."[4] During the past forty years of reform and opening up, China has been catching up to more advanced economies through industrial upgrading, encouraged and facilitated by policy and regulatory actions. But a turning point occurred in 2013, when Xi Jinping shifted the goal to that of facilitating China's emergence as a global technology leader moving towards the technological frontier. *China 2030*, a joint research report published in 2013 by the State Council's Development Research Center and the World Bank, proposed a market-based strategy to promote increased competition in all sectors, and even the withdrawal of government from direct involvement in production, distribution, and resource allocation.[5] In 2015 Xi changed direction by expanding state-led intervention with the introduction of the Made in China 2025 (MIC 2025) industrial innovation strategy. The focus shifted from market-based reform to a mixed approach relying on market forces in some areas and in others a concerted push by the state for Chinese economic dominance. Substantial public funding poured into R&D in strategic emerging sectors and AI, where experts describe China as mere steps behind the United States.[6] China has an impressive record in R&D spending,[7] and is a world leader in patents filed. But these are "input" measures when what matters are "outputs" in terms of productivity gains.

China's record of innovation that generates new ideas and commercializes them as new products varies across industries. In e-commerce and online services industries, Chinese enterprises have emerged as first movers, responding to demand from the country's huge, fast-growing, and underserved number of middle-class consumers. As discussed below, other industries have also developed unique processes to improve efficiency and speed up R&D processes. Evidence of global competitiveness is more modest, however, among China's large science- and engineering-based industrial firms, where learning and knowledge are essential for success in international markets.[8]

CHINESE INNOVATIONS IN E-COMMERCE

In China's e-commerce and digital industries, a new breed of innovator has emerged among entrepreneurs with global mindsets who are familiar with cutting-edge technologies. Over the 2014–16 period, China became one of the world's leading investors in digital technology, pouring an estimated $77 billion in venture capital into Chinese firms, representing a sixfold increase from $12 billion over the 2011–13 period.[9] Accelerating this growth was the rapid rise in domestic demand and global diffusion of new technologies. McKinsey Global Institute estimates that China now accounts for 40 per cent or more of the worldwide value of e-commerce transactions.[10] Both growing middle-class demand and the digital revolution, which facilitates input supply and product delivery, have supported scale economies in producing and paying for consumer goods and services. Insulated from foreign competition, significant parts of the Chinese market took on a life of their own. Moreover the spectacular development of online consumer markets in China still has far to run as digitalization moves beyond consumers to industrial and services producers.

China has unique advantages in such innovation. Most obvious is its 100-million-strong "consuming class," whose numbers are expected to double by 2025.[11] China also has well over 700 million Internet users (Table 2.1) supporting a vast scale of production. In such a large market, incremental innovations frequently produce more-than-incremental returns. Additionally, the size of the online population provides space for small new firms to enter the market. Chinese consumers are unusually receptive to new products and technologies. Mobile payment is a notable example of a new technology that has attracted a huge consumer response because it is easier to use than the more conventional and cumbersome credit and debit card services banks provide. As a result, China is becoming a cashless society far in advance of any other nation, with mobile payments estimated to have totalled $8.6 trillion in 2016 – in the United States that year, the total was $112 billion.[12] This preference for mobile payments has also facilitated China's development of financial technology (fintech) industries. Not surprisingly, the three original Chinese e-commerce giants – Baidu (a search engine), Alibaba (online shopping), and Tencent (social media), collectively known as BAT – have established financial affiliates to provide simple and quick payment services.

Table 2.1 Internet Users and Penetration, Selected Countries

Country	Internet Users, 2017 (millions)	Internet Penetration, 2016 (users as % of population)
China	772	52.2
India	462	34.8
United States	312	88.5
Brazil	149	66.4
Japan	119	91.1
Russia	109	71.3
Nigeria	93	46.1

Sources: Internet users: "Internet World Stats," available online at https://www.internetworldstats.com/top20.htm; Internet penetration: Internet Live Stats, "Internet Users by Country, 2016)," available online at http://www.internetlivestats.com/internet-users-by-country/.

Alibaba's Alipay runs its own digital payments business, while Yu'e Bao, a financial affiliate of BAT, provides digital wealth-management services; both are owned by Ant Financial, valued at $150 billion in a 2018 fundraising initiative.[13] Tencent developed payment services through Tenpay, online banking through WeBank, and WeChat, a multipurpose mobile app. Together these service providers control most of the mobile market in China. By 2015 as many as three new lending platforms were reported to be coming online each day – and an average of two others failed. A belated crackdown on online fraud failed, however, to prevent a collapse in P2P lending in mid-2018 because of the powerful effects of the deleveraging campaign on small borrowers and on lending platforms.

These networks of services allow users seamless movement across retail transactions and payment as well as savings and investment transactions in what is called a digital "ecosystem" that provides one-stop shopping for an ever-widening variety of goods and services available through "super apps." The conveniences provided WeChat and Alipay customers are also effectively exchanged for a treasure trove of data about their lives and preferences as they purchase increasingly diverse services ranging from tuition payments for education to physical activity tracking, news services, and entertainment. WeChat's super app includes forty functions; Alipay's has ninety.[14]

The formidable volumes of data from more than 700 million Internet users are a major source of China's emerging capabilities in AI. These data can be used by software engineers, if privacy laws permit, as inputs to the machine learning that is fundamental to artificial intelligence. In July 2017 the State Council issued a "New Generation AI Development Plan" and a roadmap for AI to become a $150 billion industry by 2030.[15] Indeed the absence of data protection laws in China is a significant facilitating factor in the development of AI tools in fields such as health care and finance, but also in the nascent "social credit" system being developed by the Chinese authorities to evaluate both financial creditworthiness and personal trustworthiness. A cyber-security law that took effect in June 2017 mandates data localization, requiring foreign firms to store their Chinese data in China and forbidding them from using these data to offer services to third parties. Such a requirement prevents non-Chinese enterprises from pooling data across countries. But, as experts point out, data are only one dimension of AI capabilities; other key dimensions include algorithms, insights, and research, which know no borders.

The volume and diversity of information on China's consumers is already providing the basis for AI applications. Baidu Medical Brain, for example, is intended to address structural problems in the health care system, such as the imbalance in available resources between rural and urban areas.[16] Newer digital entrant Xiaomi is diversifying its smartphone applications for a wider range of aspects of consumer behaviour, while NetEase, an Internet technology company with a large mobile news application, is also building a digital ecosystem.[17]

As noted, government is relatively absent from this discussion of China's burgeoning e-commerce and online activity, particularly as owner and regulator. SOEs are virtually absent from the list of large privately owned firms such as BAT, although they still predominate among listed companies. Instead, increasing numbers of privately owned enterprises appear as publicly listed companies. As recently as 2012, only 73 such firms had a market capitalization of more than US$1 billion and sufficient trading volumes; by 2017, the number had grown to 847. Many are in consumer goods, health care, and technology, while SOEs remain in traditional energy, materials, industrials, utilities, and real estate.[18]

The e-commerce example also illustrates how regulation lags innovation. Such a lag is not unique to China: explanations of the genesis of the 2008 global financial crisis prominently include the lag in the United States between the spread of financial innovations and regulators' responses. In China, regulators were absent during the first decade of online activity. Only in 2016, eleven years after Alipay introduced online money transfers, did regulators move to cap individual permitted values. Scandals erupted as some online operators developed Ponzi schemes to defraud their customers. At least two multi-billion-dollar Ponzi schemes disguised as transactions between peer-to-peer lenders, and many smaller frauds, have taken investors' funds or invested them badly. After the regulatory crackdowns began, P2P lending grew 43 per cent in outstanding loans between June 2017 and when the collapse began in June 2018.[19] The core reason to regulate commercial banks is prudential: to create incentive frameworks that ensure appropriate leverage and modern risk management by banks entrusted with household and business savings. Yet when regulators fail to understand the risks of innovative financial products, they are slow to apply the fiduciary principles of oversight. This relatively hands-off approach towards privately owned enterprises in the online industries contrasts sharply with the state's quantitative targets and interventions in manufacturing, where it aspires to become a superpower.

DELIVERING CHINESE INNOVATIONS

Sectoral studies by Cambridge University economist Peter Williamson and colleagues have contributed significant insights into Chinese innovations in new production processes and R&D to accelerate economic change. The forty cases Williamson and his colleagues look at are in a variety of industries, including e-commerce, personal computers, equipment industries for medical diagnostic devices and music equipment, pharmaceutical R&D, telecommunications equipment, mobile communication equipment, and original equipment manufacturing.[20] Their examinations show that Chinese entrepreneurs approach disruption with intention, rather than through discovery. They also argue that market managers and entrepreneurs in the developed economies need to be more alert to disruptive innovations in emerging market economies by locating there, rather than by adapting innovations from imported products. Those exposed to disruptive innovation might need to re-engineer their own processes along the lines of disruptive innovations in emerging markets, such as industrializing R&D.

Industrializing the innovation process: Williamson and colleagues' case studies show that disruptive innovations in target industries increase the efficiency of production and reduce costs. "Industrializing" the innovation processes does not rely on experimenting with new ideas by an investor or small team, nor does it involve large-scale, tightly defined processes. Instead the approach is to divide innovation into a large number of small steps and assign teams to work on each stage like an assembly line to accelerate the process of product development and the pace at which new products are brought to market. Telecom equipment manufacturer Huawei, for example, has accelerated production and reduced prices by adding many more engineers to each R&D project than would be the case in a traditional operation and organizing them into small teams, each with a specific task. Such modifications have allowed both economies of scale and specialization.

Modularizing product development: Modularization of product development is another innovative approach in which the design process is broken down into small units or modules that are then 'knitted" together by software. Design improvements are speeded up by using a "launch + test + improve" sequence. Even building construction has been modularized, as dramatically demonstrated by the Changsha-based Broad Group, which constructed a fifty-seven-storey hotel in nineteen days.[21]

Parallel processing in R&D: Another innovation is parallel processing in R&D, a technique developed by Lenovo, borrowing from the idea of parallel processing used in supercomputers, whereby, instead of using a linear process, various R&D functions that are normally sequential are conducted simultaneously. The process is reported to work well where the underlying technology is unchanged, but the production process is disruptive of costs, applications, and business model innovations.

In summary, disruptive innovations are prevalent in Chinese companies in response to intense market competition. These companies share the common characteristic of scale that enables them to make decisions more rapidly than can their smaller competitors about cost-reducing changes or changes in the business model, because even moderate success can deliver results above breakeven. Although these findings are specific to China, Williamson and colleagues conclude that international competitors should pay heed, since they might require such capabilities to be successful in the next round of global competition in developing country markets, where lower-priced products and value for money will be critical factors for success.

BECOMING A WORLD LEADER IN ADVANCED MANUFACTURING

The role of market forces is less evident in Made in China 2025, often called China's industrial policy, where the state dominates the economy to realize the goal of the country's becoming a world leader in advanced manufacturing. To that end, the state encourages local content to reduce the growing risk of relying on foreign technologies, while funding outbound investment to obtain the technology and skills required for the targeted industries. MIC 2025 is a successor to the "Medium- to Long-Term Plan for the Development of Science and Technology" adopted in 2006 with the aim of transforming China into an innovative society by 2020 and a world leader in science and technology by 2050. Seven "strategic emerging industries" – energy-efficient environmental technologies, next-generation IT, biotech, high-end equipment manufacturing, new energy, new-energy autos, and new materials[22] – were identified where China should achieve mastery through indigenous innovation, investment in R&D, accumulation of IP, and the obtaining of foreign technologies in exchange for granting access to the Chinese market.

In 2015 the Ministry of Industry and Information Technology rolled out MIC 2025, a ten-year innovation agenda influenced by Germany's Industry 4.0 strategy to become a leader in advanced manufacturing production. MIC 2025 builds on key aspects of the existing "factory of the world" ecosystem, particularly the size of the supplier base. China has five times the size of Japan's supplier base, 150 million factory workers, and good infrastructure all of which give it supply chain advantages, most spectacularly evident in the cost advantages of the solar panel industry, where China has become the world's leading producer.[23] MIC 2025 identifies ten priority sectors that overlap and expand the strategic emerging industries identified in 2006: advanced IT, robotics and automated machines, aerospace and aeronautical equipment, maritime equipment and hi-tech shipping, advanced rail transport equipment, new-energy vehicles and equipment, power and agricultural equipment, new materials, and biopharma and advanced medical products.[24]

Massive state funding is available for what appears to be a direct challenge to advanced manufacturing in the United States, East Asia, and Europe, and is intended to increase import substitution and reduce China's dependence on foreign suppliers of sophisticated equipment, particularly digital and communications equipment.[25] Domestic content has been set at 40 per cent of core components and materials by 2020, and 70 per cent by 2025. Outward investment is encouraged and supported in order to acquire core technologies through mergers and acquisitions. But the US administration's decision to label China a strategic competitor has increased the risk of China's continuing to rely on foreign technologies, and turned a spotlight on established discriminatory Chinese practices that restrict market access for foreign investors and force technology transfers in joint ventures. There are some exceptions. "Innovation demonstration zones," announced in July 2017, are intended to treat foreign and domestic investments the same except in certain sectors.[26] Market forces play a role, mainly in consumer goods and services production and distribution, where MIC 2025 calls for market institutions, stronger protection of intellectual property for small and medium-sized enterprises, more effective use of IP in business strategy, and recognition of technology standards.[27]

All levels of government in China are involved. Local governments, in particular, have pushed projects forward, speeding progress towards national goals, especially in robotics. Impressive indeed, but performance has to be weighed against evidence that funds are being misallocated and efforts duplicated in the rush. The heavy state role raises questions about the implications of such politicization for the innovation ecosystem. Will political goals and quantitative targets crowd out individual initiatives, fundraising, and risk-taking?

A careful assessment of MIC 2025 by Germany's Mercator Institute for China Studies (MERICS)[28] predicts that mismatched priorities between government and industry and overemphasis on quantitative targets, among other factors, will send mixed messages to investors. Tensions between political and economic goals are inevitable. Excessive focus on quantitative targets is likely to divert energies from bottom-up entrepreneurial innovation, and promises of generous funding will cause distortions and waste. As Barry Naughton and others have pointed out, China is ignoring the lessons of the success of Japan, South Korea, and Taiwan – particularly their decisions to reduce the role of the state to setting the economic framework, producing public goods, and improving productivity performance by freeing up market forces and promoting competition.[29]

A counterargument put forward in China is that misallocation of capital and living with excess capacity might be the acceptable costs of reaching the technological frontier. High-speed trains provide one example. To build them, firms were attracted from Japan, Canada, and France as joint venture partners and expected to share their technologies. As supply chains were localized, the Chinese partners benefited while their foreign partners lost their technological advantages and began to face their former joint venture partners as competitors. Although it is premature to predict MIC 2025's potential for success, some draw a parallel with China's experience with semiconductors. The industry was initially marked by excess capacity and lack of competitiveness, but after twenty years of effort, China has created a vast electronics base, one internationally competitive producer in Lenovo, and a largely indigenized electronics supply chain. Significantly, however, efforts to catch up and master the design and manufacture of semiconductors have yet to bear fruit – China imports more than 95 per cent of its high-end chips, and the Trump administration is using investment restrictions and export controls to slow progress.[30]

ENTERPRISE OWNERSHIP AND PRODUCTIVITY COMPARISONS IN CHINESE ENTERPRISES

Implicit in the MERICS assessment are concerns about the mixed effects of ownership on productivity performance. University of Toronto economist Loren Brandt and colleagues compare the productivity performance of SOEs and non-state firms in three different years (1998, 2007, and 2013),[31] and find evidence of a remarkable shift through time. In 1998 non-state firm productivity averaged 15 per cent higher than that of state firms, with the gap evident in 80 per cent of the sectors studied. By 2013, however, productivity was lower in non-state firms than in SOEs in a majority of sectors. Significantly, this decline in productivity coincided with the disappearance of new entrants in these industries (largely private firms) and fewer incumbent firms, raising questions about the negative effects of state intervention, such as MIC 2025, that favours domestic firms and particular sectors. This evidence also suggests a decline in state support for liberalizing policies and for deregulation to promote competition.

In another study of differential behaviour by ownership, Nicholas Lardy focuses on the recent borrowing behaviour of SOEs and privately owned enterprises. He finds that the latter's share of bank loans to non-financial corporations dropped sharply from 57 per cent of the total in 2013 to 19 per cent in 2015. In contrast the SOE share of such loans almost doubled, from 35 to 69 per cent over the same period. This trend can be expected to be exacerbated by the policy shift in 2016 towards tighter financial conditions to reduce systemic risk. Indications are that the biggest losers from tighter access to credit will be the less-well-known small and medium-sized enterprises that create most of the jobs.[32]

INNOVATION AND STATE INTERVENTION

Studies such as those of Lardy and Brandt and colleagues underline the importance of institutions for productivity performance. Government policies play a prominent role: protectionist policies that deny entry to foreign competitors in the e-commerce industry are seen as key factors in Chinese firms' success in the home market as they adapt existing (foreign) technologies. While government ministries orchestrate strategic plans for China to become an innovative society, tensions are apparent between the Party's primary concern to preserve political and economic stability and the economic freedoms and openness associated with a vibrant market economy. Seasoned outsiders and China watchers have warned of the potentially negative implications of this ambiguity. Henry Paulson, former Goldman Sachs chairman and US treasury secretary, observes in his book, *Dealing with China*, that success in an innovation-rich economy is driven by human ingenuity that thrives on free and open exchange: "You can't run a successful business cut off from the world."[33] In a 2014 *Harvard Business Review* article, "Why China Can't Innovate,"[34] the authors argue that China has been successful with creative adaptation but has not led. The problem, they assert, is not innovative or intellectual capacity, but the restrictive political framework in which business and education must operate, which is "very much bounded."

A number of other studies show that state intervention is successful in industries in which enterprises rely on substantial accumulation of knowledge and engineering skills. High-speed trains, mentioned above, are an example of state ownership and support, both to increase local demand and to negotiate joint venture agreements with foreign producers. China's share of the global market for such trains is now 41 per cent. Wind power and communications equipment provide other examples featuring Chinese producers. In wind power, the original approach was to allow open bidding, which led to a flood of foreign imports. In response, SOEs were required to source 70 per cent of their components from domestic suppliers. These policies forced the creation of joint ventures in local production and diffused knowledge from foreign producers to local firms. By 2009 six of the ten top wind power firms were Chinese, and by 2010 they accounted for 93 per cent of world sales. The state has also helped them acquire knowledge through high-profile programs such as the 2003 Wind Power Concession Project.[35]

Science-based innovation is another priority area where state investments are being used to build institutions and capabilities, notably in pharmaceuticals, biotech, semiconductor design, and specialty chemicals. Such innovation takes a long time to pay off, and is hampered by slow regulatory processes, IP protection, inefficient allocation of government funding, and underinvestment by the private sector. But some Chinese firms in drug discovery are successfully using the accelerated innovation models of Williamson and colleagues.[36]

In telecommunications, in contrast, Huawei Technologies provides an example of the opposite behaviour: its response was to globalize. In this case, however, foreign partners were reluctant to share their cutting-edge technologies, and state support was not forthcoming. Huawei had to invest in developing its technology through expensive trial-and-error processes, but it eventually succeeded in creating its own sophisticated designs, albeit with R&D expenditures totalling 12 per cent of revenue. The strategy also included localizing innovation among centres situated around the world.[37]

As noted, China has not achieved its goals for the design and manufacture of semiconductors and semiconductor equipment, but continues to depend on foreign technologies and IP. The United States, the still-undisputed industry leader, has screened foreign bids for US firms in order to deny Chinese investors access to key technologies. In response China is now investing heavily in state-funded research through MIC 2025 and other state plans to develop a world-class semiconductor industry. Its reported aim is to produce 40 per cent of its requirements for semiconductors by 2020, up from 16 per cent in 2018.[38] Foreign governments are now moving to protect their own competitiveness – for example, recent US legislation authorizes export controls of critical technologies and expands the scope and rigour of interagency reviews by the Committee on Foreign Investment in the United States (CFIUS) of commercial transactions in order to protect core technologies.

Finally, educational institutions are playing a critical role in China's innovation future. Performance indicators are positive, as measured by the rapid expansion of higher education investments and enrolments and the recognition in global rankings of China's investments in university education and evidence of rising quality of education. In 2015 nearly 37 million students were enrolled in higher education, up from 24 million in 2012.[39] Support for university education has been significantly ramped up, turning out 6.8 million graduates in 2015, up from half that number in 2005.[40] Offsetting this part of the picture, however, are two problematic factors: one is that many Chinese graduates fail to remain in the country, preferring to leave to study or do research abroad; the other is that the state has been tightening restrictions on content to rely more on national sources and institutions.

GLOBAL IMPLICATIONS

What are the implications of these various state roles in China's innovation performance? First, China has a huge advantage of scale in developing digital services, AI, and machine learning in industries of the future. Looking ahead, the surge in digital services is providing the abundant processing power and data that, along with the rapid growth of available technical talent, are needed at the AI research frontier the Chinese government seeks.[41] A problematic feature of this surge, however, is the data-localization requirement the government imposed in June 2017. In strategic terms, restricting such significant technologies to Chinese institutions prevents foreign competitors from being active in the Chinese market, and it protects Chinese IP. But it also reduces the likelihood that Chinese AI researchers, for example, will be permitted to work with foreign technology companies to develop global safety standards. The application of Chinese AI technologies such as facial recognition to public surveillance and security screening also raises questions about the differential treatment of privacy in China and abroad.

A second issue with global implications relates to China's learning about and acquiring new technologies through outward FDI and mergers and acquisitions (see Chapter 4). Many of the enterprises involved are SMEs and job creators as well as entrepreneurial leaders among privately owned enterprises in a range of industries that the Chinese government has encouraged to obtain foreign technology through joint ventures with and acquisitions of foreign companies – and by controversial means such as forced technology transfers. Between 2013 and 2015, outward mergers and acquisitions surged in technology-based industries, and some Chinese technology firms located R&D centres abroad. Huawei has 16 R&D centres around the world while Haier and Sany have done the same.[42] Lack of reciprocal market access for US investors seeking to enter the Chinese market, together with the rising public profile of the state-supported MIC 2025, has, as noted, prompted stepped up US scrutiny of Chinese investment in the United States and export controls of critical technologies.

The third, and related, issue is outright Chinese theft of IP from both US and European sources. In a 2017 report, the Blair-Huntsman bipartisan Commission on the Theft of American Intellectual Property published estimates of the cost of stolen trade secrets in the hundreds of billions of dollars, particularly in biotechnology.[43] Critics, however, argue that such numbers are likely inflated by including perfectly legal scientific cooperation. Further, recent reports of US patent recipients show Chinese inventors receiving 11,241 patents in fiscal year 2016/17, a 28 per cent increase in a year, but still only 3.5 per cent of the total number of 320,003 patents issued that year. Huawei alone had received nearly 1,500 patents by the end of 2017,[44] showing that electronic manufacturers are beginning to develop their own technologies and branded products.

Other data, however, show evidence of a growing market for the purchase of intellectual property in the United States. Nicholas Lardy has pointed out that, rather than theft or forced foreign technology transfers from multinational companies, China's payments for foreign IP have risen rapidly, reaching almost $30 billion in 2017, ranking it as the fourth-largest acquirer, behind Ireland, the Netherlands, and the United States.[45]

In summary, China is emerging as a dynamic and ambitious player in technological innovation. It has the unique advantages of the swift adoption of smartphones, rapid related software development and e-commerce, and the huge market size and scale of its customer base. Investment bankers are increasingly impressed by the speed and scale of movement by dynamic Chinese entrepreneurs into fintech, biotechnology, and AI, and their focus on innovation in operating models and services, rather than on more traditional product innovation.[46] Chinese entrepreneurs are also seeking growth opportunities in the rest of the world, often with official support and encouragement. Their success in customer-focused innovation at home can be extended to emerging market economies if Chinese enterprises can develop the necessary sales and marketing skills. Chinese examples of disruptive innovation also have relevance for those who can apply them in both advanced and emerging market economies.

CONCLUSION

Is China becoming the "leading technology innovator" proclaimed by the *South China Morning Post*? Such a query is helpful in framing the issue more broadly. As noted earlier, there are differing views of Chinese innovation capabilities. Those who point to evidence of Chinese capabilities and their distinctive approaches argue there is even a Chinese model of innovation. Others argue that China's innovation capabilities are constrained by the underlying tensions between state and market, as indicated by industry-level data on ownership and productivity, forcing China to continue to rely on foreign sources for innovative technologies.

Size matters. China can afford failures on the road to success. Even incremental change in the huge Chinese market can have major effects, and already China has a record of notable achievement in e-commerce, consumer services, and, increasingly, financial services. Not to be overlooked, however, is the protection these sectors enjoy from competition with foreign entrants. Services – including finance, telecommunications, transportation, and media, each of which is dominated by less-productive SOEs – are largely closed to foreign investment, yet they are also among the fastest growing sectors as the economy rebalances. Opening this and other sectors to foreign competition, skills, and technologies could be growth promoting.

Key institutional concerns remain. State support for advanced manufacturing raises questions about the global future of industries populated by oversized SOEs with problematic competitiveness. Until the significant tensions between political and economic objectives inherent in SOEs' incentive structures are resolved, we are unlikely to see modern-day Chinese innovations as important as gunpowder and the compass; continued adaptation is likely to be the rule, rather than the exception. Instead, as recent analyses by Nicholas Lardy and Brandt and colleagues suggest, unless the model of state-led capitalism is eased, it could undermine China's long-term economic potential. Such evidence raises doubts about the *South China Post's* optimistic prediction. The policy environment and incentive frameworks in China are sending mixed signals about the roles of the market and the state. MIC 2025 sends a clear message that the state knows best how to reach the technological frontier. The state still believes in top-down targets and quantitative evaluations, rather than in bottom-up innovation in response to market-based incentives – although there is encouraging evidence of breakthroughs in some Chinese industries. More evidence is required of market opening, measures to attract investment, and increased protection for intellectual property. The adoption of a new FDI law in March 2019 by National People's Congress is a positive development, although the regulations to implement the law have yet to be written. That is when differences over the role of the state will become clearer.

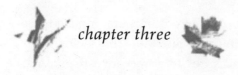

chapter three

CREATING A LEADING FINANCIAL SYSTEM: A WORK IN PROGRESS

In October 2017, during the 19th Party Congress, Zhou Xiaochuan, one of China's most respected economic leaders, who would retire in 2018 after a fifteen-year tenure as governor of China's central bank, issued a stark warning about the risks China faced from "excessive debt and speculative investment." He spoke of a possible sharp correction, known as a "Minsky moment," so named for US economist Hyman Minsky, who became well known for suggesting that financial risks previously ignored or hidden during an economic expansion could surface unexpectedly, causing asset prices to drop, followed by financial defaults with potential systemic consequences. Indeed, official concern about systemic financial risk had been growing in the leadup to the Party Congress. Multiple factors contributed to official intervention: the confluence in 2015–16 of a negative growth shock, a major stock market boom and bust, a surge in capital outflows to pay for large foreign acquisitions of non-core assets by private enterprises, and associated exchange-rate depreciation. Corporate enterprises were ordered to reduce their indebtedness, banks were ordered to write off bad loans that had accumulated on – and significantly – off their books. Banking and insurance regulators who had operated in silos were merged, replaced with a common supervisory framework to prevent financial risks and manage them if they occurred.

Zhou's warnings, however, were about a financial system that is a work in progress – a bank-dominated system in which mandates, capabilities, and skills in financial regulatory institutions lag financial innovation and risk-taking in the economy. It is a system conveying mixed signals from political leaders who focused on aggregate growth targets, to be met if necessary by expanding credit, even if such a move magnified liquidity concerns. Only belatedly did their focus shift to preventing and managing the systemic risks of "excessive debt and speculative investment." China's financial system and its institutions are rooted in the planned economy, but a modern financial system is based on transparency and the rule of law, which are necessary to manage the volatility introduced by cross-border financial flows. The institutions of the modern financial system supply short-term credit through banks and Internet finance, and long-term direct finance through bond and equities markets. Inevitably, as China's economy grows, its financial system will become deeply integrated into world markets. How might China proceed as its financial institutions and regulatory practices continue to develop and change, and what are the risks of financial crisis in light of ongoing modernization and opening up?

Background

A modern financial system, first and foremost, should support the real economy. It does so by reducing information asymmetries between borrowers, who know a lot about their ability to repay loans on time and in full, and lenders, who do not. A modern system facilitates payments in economic exchange, mobilizes and pools savings, acquires and processes information about potential investments, helps direct savings to productive uses, diversifies and reduces risk, and monitors investments in enterprises as well as the performance of their managers.

China started down this road following its accession to the World Trade Organization (WTO) in 2001, when the banking system was opened and modernized. International investors were attracted by opportunities to acquire stakes in large state-owned banks to help them upgrade their management and introduce market discipline through public listings of their shares. Separate banking, insurance, and securities regulators provided regulatory oversight. Interest rates, initially set by the State Council, were eventually liberalized to improve the pricing of risk. At the same time, regulators tolerated the proliferation of new wealth-management products and trust loans. Other non-bank financial institutions were also attracted by this relatively lighter regulation, and used banks' branch networks to expand their own supply networks to sell these new products, thereby further expanding credit.

Following the 2008–09 financial crisis, the state injected stimulus through bank loans, rather than through government spending. The removal of credit controls and other restrictions and the approval of an infrastructure spending program resulted in significant loan growth through both bank and non-bank channels. The authorities also set quantitative growth targets in order to maintain employment and economic growth. This emphasis sent mixed signals about the role of market forces and official support for growth by encouraging lending by state-owned banks to SOEs and provincial and municipal governments. Regulators operating in silos failed, however, to provide a consistent incentive framework in the fast-growing and evolving economy. Rather than sharing their goals and priorities or coordinating their actions, regulators competed with one another, creating conditions for regulatory arbitrage and failing to keep abreast of financial innovations.[1] The risk of financial insecurity led to a reform blitz by China's leaders and warnings from both the IMF and the Bank for International Settlements. The latter estimated that, in 2017,

China's debt overhang had reached dangerous levels, with official total debt exceeding 260 per cent of GDP, non-financial sector debt at 235 per cent of GDP, and private sector debt at 175 per cent of GDP.[2] By mid-year 2017, Moody's had downgraded its rating of China's sovereign debt from Aa3 to A1.

Governor Zhou had argued for modernizing the relatively closed financial sector and integrating it into world markets as a way to achieve China's long-term growth and rebalancing objectives. Consistent with China's becoming a leading economy, he argued for the long-term goal of an internationalized renminbi that would follow the completion of carefully sequenced financial reforms – including strengthening financial institutions so that they could withstand the inevitable increases in market volatility as protectionist barriers to cross-border financial flows were removed. Other reforms would allow the exchange rate and interest rates, as key prices, to be determined by market forces, rather than by political decision. These and other reforms would also promote transparency, the rule of law, and modern accounting practices. The IMF decision in October 2016 to add the renminbi to its currency basket making up the Special Drawing Right, the IMF's unit of account, was a significant step along this road[3] and seen as affirming China's economic potential. To Chinese policymakers, it was an important step towards expanding the use of the renminbi beyond a unit of account in settling international transactions to become a means of payment and eventually a store of value for banks, enterprises, and governments around the world.

Renminbi internationalization would have other potential benefits. Increasing renminbi-denominated trade finance would reduce dependence on the US dollar and the costs of seigniorage.[4] But there would be risks. Allowing cross-border transactions would expose the economy to market volatility, which would have to be managed. Strong supervisory oversight and coordination among regulators would be required. Property rights would need to be protected. Changing the incentive structure would free up market forces and encourage a wider range of financial instruments for savings and investment. Short-term bank financing, which had long dominated the Chinese system, would have to be augmented by long-term finance from transparent, sound, and credible bond and equity markets. The banking deposit insurance system introduced in 2015 would have to discipline risk-taking by removing a major source of moral hazard, since lenders could no longer count on government to assume the risks and bail them out of bad decisions. All these features are precursors to the fully open capital account necessary for full internationalization.

In 2016–17 heightened concerns about the possible systemic effects of financial risk on national security and on growth targets deflected the official focus to fighting fires in the leadup to the 19th Party Congress. One of these fires was the increased capital outflows associated with the wave of large offshore corporate mergers and acquisitions transactions in the previous year (see Chapter 4). In several cases, acquisitions were considered risky because they were outside the core expertise of the enterprise; others, such as of hotels, entertainment, and real estate entities, were "frivolous" in that they did not contribute to national growth objectives. The wave of transactions in 2016 also exacerbated the market weakness of the renminbi at a time when the authorities sought to support its value. In response, rather than accept market forces and support the currency, the authorities chose to intervene with capital controls to support domestic objectives, adding to risk and market confusion. Yu Yongding, a former member of the central bank's monetary policy committee, publicly criticized official indecision about establishing and sticking to, an exchange-rate rule and confusing market participants about central bank intentions towards a market-determined and more flexible exchange rate.[5] In other words, renminbi internationalization was not to be – at least not yet.

BANKS, SHADOW BANKS, AND REGULATORY ARBITRAGE

Banks are a big part of the picture of China's excessive debt and spec-ulative investment problem because of regulators' tolerance of the buildup of off-balance-sheet activities. At the time of its accession to the WTO in 2001, China had negotiated a five-year window for its banks to learn to compete with foreigners. Chinese banks trans-ferred large stocks of legacy non-performing loans from their books to those of state-financed asset management corporations charged with collecting or calling the loans. The four large state-owned com-mercial banks listed their shares on stock exchanges, and accepted strategic investments from foreign banks limited to 25 per cent of their equity. All of these steps were designed to change the incen-tive framework for bank boards and managers to respond to market forces and to become more transparent to market monitoring.

By 2017 the strategic investors had sold their shares (at consid-erable profit), further foreign investment in the financial sector had been discouraged, and much work remained to introduce market forces into the banking sector. The state-owned commercial banks had become accustomed to fixed interest rates and a generous spread between deposit and lending rates, which allowed them riskless income. Expertise to manage risk was also lacking. The small and medium-sized enterprises that create most of China's jobs had difficulty accessing bank credit in the absence of incentives for the commercial banks to take on such risky, unconnected customers.

The four state-owned commercial banks are also the world's largest banks as measured by tier one capital – the measure regu-lators use of a bank's financial strength, which consists mainly of equity and retained earnings. Ownership reform is recognized as a necessary objective, but rather than make shares available to the public and to private investors, the government chose to encour-age the growth of multiple smaller financial institutions, includ-ing rural banks, banking and credit cooperatives, new financing institutions, and private banks, eleven of which received licences in 2016. Although market forces now play a larger role in determining interest rates, state-owned commercial banks continue to rely on SOEs as major customers, along with local governments and other large, well-known, low-risk corporate clients.

In this environment of credit market distortions and inconsistent regulatory frameworks, off-balance-sheet credit creations – known as shadow banking – proliferated. These products create credit using either entrusted loans between companies – transactions in which banks serve only as middle men and take on no risk; or trust loans – where banks serve as a conduit for the proceeds of wealth-management products to invest in a trust plan used by corporate borrowers. Starved for financing from reluctant state-owned banks, small and medium-sized enterprises were among the major customers of these loans.

Shadow banking in turn created distortions that initially escaped regulators' scrutiny. Bank depositors and customers searching for higher-yield products and higher rates of return sought these non-bank off-balance-sheet credit products because they were largely beyond regulatory purview. As shadow banking became entrenched, these practices spread to financial institutions, which began to lend to one another, and then to the regulators themselves, who began to compete with one another to attract this business. In this way, the problem grew beyond the banking system into the insurance and equities sectors as well.

Burgeoning demand for these unregulated products created new risks of corporate leverage, which were magnified by the popular practice of securitizing the loans and bundling them into products for which no institution seemed liable. Moral hazard was rampant as financial market participants took more risks, assuming the state would bail them out and reduce the consequences of bad investment choices. A comparative study shows, however, that the scale of China's shadow banking activities is moderate by global standards – at an estimated 10–27 per cent of bank assets in 2012, compared with a global average of 61 per cent.[6] The government's 2017 campaign against financial leverage curbed both lending and bond financing, creating a credit crunch for privately owned enterprises of a severity that, by mid-2018, required a range of actions by the central bank, beginning with the expansion of short-term credit facilities.

The central bank and regulators also took significant coordinated steps in 2017 and 2018, issuing new draft rules to curtail shadow banking by eliminating implicit guarantees and reducing opportunities for regulatory arbitrage and maturity mismatch in asset management. These rules have important implications. First, the incentive system has been changed by merging the banking and insurance regulators into the China Banking and Insurance Regulatory Commission (CBIRC), with one set of rules, thereby discouraging or eliminating regulatory arbitrage. Second, the new rules shift risk to investors from people and institutions. Asset managers will be required to manage transparent portfolios of assets, instead of offering products promising high returns as riskless as a bank deposit. Banks were ordered to bring off-balance-sheet loans back onto their books as a way of returning such activities to them.[7] As a result, banks wrote off $780 billion in bad loans and raised substantial quantities of new capital.[8] In December 2018, the CBIRC announced that commercial lenders would have to separate their wealth-management subsidiaries into independent operations, effectively abolishing the soft guarantees for loans that had been the main attraction. By the end of 2020, wealth-management products will be marked to market – that is, valuing the wealth-management product at current market prices.[9] As well, loan-provisioning requirements have been adjusted to encourage recognition of non-performing loans. In 2018, the IMF noted that the size of China's shadow banking sector had declined, as had interconnections between banks and non-banks.[10]

THE RISE OF DIGITAL FINANCE AND FINTECH

Even as financial institutions gradually increase their efficiency and regulators improve and modernize oversight, the new opportunities and risks of the digital revolution have introduced disruptive change to credit markets. As noted in the previous chapter, China's more than 700 million Internet and mobile device users provide unique scale opportunities for innovation. Computer programs and other technology used to support or enable banking and financial services – "fintech" – have grown rapidly. Morgan Stanley estimates that China now has the world's largest e-commerce market, accounting for 35 per cent of the global total in 2013; more recent estimates put the share close to 40 per cent.[11] On Singles Day 2018, Alibaba's e-commerce sales reportedly totalled US$30.8 billion in twenty-four hours.[12]

The rise of fintech seems in retrospect to have been inevitable, given the technological, regulatory, and geographic constraints of China's traditional banks and their heavy focus on large corporate borrowers and middle-class home owners. Customers were looking for low-cost finance; fintech innovations made it possible for services to respond to customers directly. The breath-taking pace and magnitude of growth in online payments and other financial transactions has led to proliferating mobile applications in consumer finance. Fintech companies are now experimenting with big data in the effort to speed up credit approval based on better customer credit profiles, and are pursuing the underbanked among students, rural households, and blue-collar workers. Customers in micro, small, and medium-sized businesses are also attracted by improvements in credit assessments.

All of these developments signal intensifying competition in financial and consumer goods markets. More competition will spur further innovation, more efficient services, and new products, such as wealth-management applications that allow middle-class savers to manage their own investments. Traditional financial institutions are cooperating with fintech firms in finding innovative, easier, and lower-cost alternatives to their traditional offerings. These e-commerce and fintech innovations, moreover, are still in their early stages. The key will be to excel in providing customer services.

Fintech, however, presents two big challenges. One is fraud. Fintech and e-commerce are vulnerable to operators who fail to deliver authentic goods – or to deliver at all; others engage in fraudulent financial practices. With growing evidence of fraud and illegal fundraising, as well as the high-profile P2P failures in mid-2018 – despite efforts to improve standards and oversight of P2P lending – more and more effective oversight is clearly required.

The second and related challenge is regulatory. A proliferation of IT companies now provide financial services such as lending and payment services and sales of insurance products, but only some of these are licensed. A modern banking system requires prudential regulation of entities that engage in asset management in order to control risk and protect depositors' balances where these are permitted. Despite the work of task forces headed by the People's Bank of China since 2016, more effective measures are still required to reduce risk in the online financial sector and, as the central bank has noted, to oversee financial technology in recognition of the speed at which the industry and cross-sector financial risks are growing.

DEVELOPING CAPITAL MARKETS AND DIRECT FINANCE

China's capital markets are being reformed to make them more open and contestable. Government intervention still occurs, sometimes alarming market participants. This was the case in 2015, when the authorities attempted to halt a collapse in stock prices by banning sales and short selling and by injecting liquidity into the market to prop up indices, which created substantial confusion and un-certainty. Even so, equity markets have been further strengthened by reducing restrictions on foreign investors engaging in China in renminbi transactions. The creation of cross-border investment channels through stock exchanges in Hong Kong, Shenzhen, and Shanghai have enabled investors in these markets to trade on one another's markets through their own brokers and clearing houses. Restrictions were also eased on short selling, and institutional margin financing was launched to enhance market depth and boost hedge fund operations.

China's bond market, now the world's third largest, is also being modernized and opened. Previously restricted to qualified foreign investors in the interbank market, the creation of the Bond Connect link with Hong Kong in 2017 facilitated cross-border investment through financial infrastructure institutions. Moves are also under way to provide direct finance to non-state enterprises. Until recently most corporate bonds were issued by SOEs in transactions largely confined to the interbank market through banks' fixed-income departments. Foreign participation was tightly controlled by quotas and licensing restrictions imposed on institutional investors. But in February 2016 the interbank market was thrown open to foreign institutions, including central banks. Surprisingly, however, financial institutions displayed little interest in this liberalization – by December, the foreign share was a mere 1.3 per cent of total market value.[13] After the disruptive official intervention in mid-2015, foreign investors remained concerned about future government interventions and capital restrictions – as occurred in June 2017.

Since 2014 concerns have also increased about default risks by both state-owned and non-state enterprises. Bond defaults are relatively rare in China, but a high-profile default in March 2014 by private solar panel manufacturer Chaori damaged expectations. A regulatory crackdown in early 2017 squeezed the money market, abruptly raising funding costs for mid-sized companies. Thirteen defaults, including by Dalian Machine Tool Group, occurred in the first half of that year as companies were unable to service their debts, causing concerns about contagion due to the widespread practice of companies guaranteeing each other's loans.[14] By mid-2018 the bond market set a new record for defaults, which increased the cost of credit.

Long experience in other countries has shown that allowing defaults, rather than intervening to save companies, reduces moral hazard and can provide a welcome reduction in accumulated debt and a means of pricing risk more accurately. Indeed, that appears to be happening. The China Securities Regulatory Commission has identified a number of desirable reforms to speed up bond market development, including a unified regulatory framework to replace fragmentation among regulators and calls for clear approval procedures, disclosure rules for bond issuers, an improved credit-rating system, clearer and enforced penalties for violators, buyer education, an interconnected trading and settlement system, and encouragement of product innovation.[15] These reforms also indicate, however, the distance the Chinese economy still has to travel to achieve market depth and soundness. With its market now one of the world's largest, China has an opportunity to continue to open its bond markets and promote accurate risk pricing as part of the transition to an economy that is less debt- and bank-dependent. Regulatory and other reforms must keep pace.[16]

RISK OF A FINANCIAL CRISIS?

Will China's significant debt overhang result in widespread default and bank runs? Given the direction of policy and institutional changes, it appears things are moving in the right direction and default risk has declined. Interest-rate deregulation is particularly significant because of the direct positive effects on household income from higher deposit rates. At the same time, however, the effect on lending rates is to increase the cost of capital for capital-intensive goods manufacturers.[17] China has abundant liquidity: the state owns most lenders and borrowers. China does not have a balance-of-payments problem, domestic funding shortfalls, or an asset bubble. Both macroeconomic management and financial regulation are relatively sound. Weaknesses tend to be localized in certain parts of the country and in certain institutions, such as the smaller state-owned banks. As noted earlier, in 2017 the IMF reported that China's ratio of total non-financial sector debt to GDP was 235 per cent, up from 207 per cent in 2014. This is cause for concern since the debt has built up rapidly as private companies shift from equity to debt offered by the unregulated financial institutions. Excess capacity has opened up in traditional industrial sectors such as coal and iron-related activity in the supply chains of infrastructure and construction industries integral to China's real estate boom. As some analysts have argued, however, China's problem is not solvency or liquidity, but capital allocation, and it is mainly a problem of SOEs in debt to state-owned commercial banks. Balance could be restored by shifting from debt to equity through state-approved debt-to-equity swaps.[18] The debt/equity imbalance could also be managed by raising more equity.

Some in China ask whether the country is headed down the same road as Japan, whose total debt-to-GDP ratio is similar in size to China's. Many analysts agree that China's debt problem differs in that it is not fed by public sector borrowing monetized by the central bank (which can be self-perpetuating); China's lenders are commercial banks that rely on deposits. This means, however, that a crisis could be triggered if defaults in the non-bank financial sector overwhelmed smaller banks and caused a bank run that froze the inter-bank market, and sentiment turned negative. Although the People's Bank of China likely would provide emergency liquidity, the disruption in credit flows would feed quickly through to investment decisions and might also trigger capital outflows,[19] threatening national security, as President Xi concluded in 2017. More desirable would be adjustments that avoided such outcomes.

FINANCIAL REGULATION REFORM

Regulatory reform became a high priority when the National Financial Work Conference decided in July 2017 to create a high-level Financial Stability and Development Commission reporting to the State Council, chaired by Vice Premier Liu He, and supported by a secretariat located at the People's Bank of China. Initially its focus was non-bank lenders, Internet finance, asset management, and financial holding companies, all of which are institutions that facilitated the growth in indebtedness.

Official momentum towards proactive financial sector adjustment picked up steam in 2016–17 once the Politburo signalled the urgency of containing leverage and financial risk. Marked tightening of financial supervision occurred in early 2017 with the promulgation of new regulatory rules in mid-2017. The central bank led the way by tightening liquidity, significantly changing supervisory requirements, and adding shadow bank off-balance-sheet wealth management products to its macro-prudential assessment. Providing a clearer picture of systemic prudential risk, however, had a markedly negative effect on expectations: interest rates rose, accompanied by a credit market sell-off. In June 2017, the central bank moved to moderate sentiment by injecting $53 billion into the banking system; regulators also adjusted the pace of their tighter scrutiny and improved coordination among themselves. As growth continued to slow in 2018, the central bank took a number of other measures. It cut banks' required reserve ratios, and offered a further $74 billion of medium-term credit of short maturity in an effort to relieve funding pressures on private sector borrowers caused by the contraction of shadow banking credit, the downgrading of smaller lenders, bond defaults, and pressures to repay dollar debt.

CONCLUSION

Proactive financial market reforms by the Chinese government have reduced the risk of a Minsky moment, but more remains to be done. Mortgage lending and shadow banking are still concerns following China's lengthy property market boom. The high-level Financial Stability and Development Commission now has a mandate to promote financial stability and coordinate financial oversight across all financial regulators as well as the central bank – as would be expected of a modern financial system.

The People's Bank of China's decision to establish Nets Union Clearing Corp. (NUCC), a central clearing platform, and issue appropriate regulation and supervision of online finance is another promising step. NUCC, which became fully operational on 1 July 2018, is now the national platform for processing online transactions undertaken by all third-party payments providers that involve bank accounts. Until then, such transactions among these third-party firms or with banks had escaped regulatory oversight. The platform also brings all online transaction data under the supervision and regulation of the central bank.[20]

These are significant developments, but uncertainty among investors about China's growth prospects persists, as reflected in the Moody's June 2017 downgrade. There remains substantial ambiguity about the relative roles of the state and market forces in the functioning of the financial system. The future of renminbi internationalization, capital account opening, and China's integration into the global financial system are other sources of uncertainty, along with rising tensions with the United States over trade and investment. Given the size of China's financial system, domestic developments and disruptions will affect its international transactions, cross-border trade, and financial flows.

President Xi's speech to the Boao Forum for Asia in April 2018 signalled China's intention to introduce significant reforms and market opening in the financial sector, further exchange-rate regime reform, and moves toward capital account convertibility and increased regulatory capacity. The next day, central bank governor Yi Gang announced further financial sector opening and changes in FDI policy, which became part of the FDI law adopted by the National People's Congress in March 2019. These changes include permission for the pre-establishment of national treatment of foreign investors, the adoption of a negative list – whereby access is permitted in all sectors except those on the list – actions to open the financial sector further to foreign participation by changing ownership regulations, and the removal of foreign ownership caps for banks and asset-management companies. The foreign ownership limit of securities companies, life insurers, and others has been increased to 51 per cent, and will be removed entirely. Joint-funded securities companies are also now allowed.

Other measures to open up the sector include increasing the daily quotas of Shanghai, Hong Kong, and Shenzhen cross-border investment flows to increase stock market connectivity; ownership changes to permit eligible foreign investors to provide insurance and loss-adjustment services in China; and national treatment of foreign-invested insurance brokerage companies. Governor Yi promised further removal of ownership restrictions in a number of financial sectors, along with commitments to permit foreign banks and securities companies to expand their business scope and to ease restrictions on insurance companies wishing to enter the Chinese market.[21]

In late 2018, following speeches by Xi Jinping and Liu He, further new measures were introduced "to improve the business environment" by easing available funding for private enterprises, small and medium-sized enterprises, and micro-enterprises. The State Administration of Taxation followed up with measures to reduce the tax burden. The People's Bank of China outlined a "1-2-5" policy directing that at least one-third of new corporate loans from large banks go to private firms, two-thirds of new loans by smaller banks go to private firms, and at least half of all new corporate credit from banks to go to the private sector for the next three years.[22] As well, a negative list of sectors closed to foreign investors was published as part of the effort to increase competitive dynamics, and administrative and tax burdens were simplified. These commitments conveyed official concerns about the erosion of private property rights and the crowding out of investment by the state that had been ignored since the Third Plenum dictum that the market will decide the allocation of resources. The persistence of state subsidies to uncompetitive state companies and the dominant state role in MIC 2025 still send conflicting signals. As some analysts have argued,[23] China's leaders seem to have accepted reduced profitability, slower growth, and the heightened financial risks of high leverage as part of the price of maintaining the Party's position and achieving the state's strategic objectives.

Finally, even as the chances of a Minsky moment diminish and renminbi internationalization is delayed, a new source of uncertainty and volatility has appeared. China's large current account surplus is shrinking – from 10 per cent of GDP in 2007 to 0.4 per cent in 2018 – as its rebalancing strategy increases consumption relative to investment.[24] This change means that Chinese demand for US financial assets such as US Treasury bonds will shrink at the same time as US financing requirements expand with the growth of the fiscal deficit. In short, US reliance on Chinese demand for Treasury bonds will increase just as that demand shrinks. The United States might be about to face some hard choices.

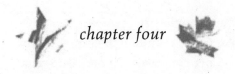

chapter four

China Invests Abroad: A New Era of Chinese Capital

China's outward direct foreign investment and mergers and acquisitions transactions boomed over the 2015–17 period, signalling a new era of capital and competition in the country's long game to become a global power. By 2016 China ranked second to the United States in outward FDI; by 2017 its accumulated stock of assets, at $1.5 trillion, equalled its stock of inward FDI from the rest of the world.[1]

China's history as an investment destination is well known, as is its outward investment record. Prior to its accession to the WTO in 2001, China sought foreign investment as a way to address domestic capital shortages. Investment approvals were case-by-case and restricted to activities that served the national interest. Outward investment was restricted and heavily regulated, totalling a mere $27 billion in 1999. WTO accession signalled Chinese enterprises to "go out" to increase their global competitiveness and access natural resources and technical expertise as part of the national investment-led, export-oriented growth strategy. The registration and approval of outward FDI was streamlined, and thresholds for investments in natural resource development projects were raised above those for other projects. Following the 2008–09 global financial crisis, investors took advantage of depressed asset prices abroad to acquire a wider range of foreign assets. As rebalancing slowed domestic growth in response, Chinese enterprises were motivated to seek new markets and foreign assets to maintain their growth. In 2016 outflows of FDI surged by 45 per cent over the previous year to $196.2 billion. With 13 per cent of the global total, China became the single most important home country and host economy among the emerging market economies.

Surging capital outflows attracted criticism and backlash, however, both in China and abroad. In China the outflows caused unanticipated exchange-rate depreciation and pressures on the capital account, undermining national development objectives. As noted in the previous chapter, a number of high-profile acquisitions of US entertainment and tourism enterprises – deemed by the authorities to be passive assets and "frivolous" acquisitions – helped to frustrate China's investment objective to obtain natural resources and acquire knowledge and technologies. Foreigners also reacted warily to the rapid increase in Chinese acquisitions and the state's active role in supporting Chinese investors seeking technology assets. Beginning in late 2016, Beijing cracked down on outward FDI, focusing in particular on that by highly leveraged privately owned enterprises.

To put this shift in context, one study finds that trade-related motives were prominent factors both in supporting China's role as the top-ranked merchandise exporter among emerging market economies and in hedging against the erection of trade barriers against those exports.[2] These motivations are evident in China's growing presence in Africa and other areas where natural resources are found. Africans have been prominent partners as China has invested heavily in raw materials to take advantage of the major growth opportunities in that continent's emerging market economies. To that end, in October 2018, at the seventh annual China-Africa Cooperation Forum, President Xi announced $60 billion in financial support for Africa.

As Chinese wages and production costs rose, efficiency-seeking investments gained in importance, as did projects to access technology, brands, and distribution networks. Chinese investors also sought to evade domestic regulatory restrictions or to gain financial advantage through round tripping and using outward FDI as a pretext to transfer financial wealth abroad.

Structural policies also influenced the growth of deals. Global financial advisory firms such as PwC and JP Morgan, close followers of trends in China's outbound mergers and acquisitions,[3] identified several such trends, including the emphasis on long-term sustainable (slower) growth, rising middle-class consumption, and more liberal and streamlined procedures in the regulatory and financial environments. Availability of competitive financing was another encouraging factor, as was the desire to hedge against a depreciating renminbi.

In late 2016, however, the investment atmosphere changed abruptly as the Party leadership became increasingly concerned about the systemic effects of rising corporate indebtedness and the effects on the exchange rate of the 45 per cent surge in capital outflows that year. Official scrutiny increasingly focused on some of the very large transactions completed earlier in the year, which had put downward pressure on the currency and drained foreign exchange reserves – sensitive issues in the wake of the serious financial volatility of 2015 and the large depreciation of the renminbi.

The China Banking and Insurance Regulatory Commission ordered banks to re-evaluate loans to "some large entities" that had made large foreign acquisitions in 2016 and earlier. Three borrowers, Anbang Insurance Group, Dalian Wanda Group, and HNA Group, were singled out for closer scrutiny of their credit exposures. Acquisitions of businesses unrelated to their core businesses or stated objectives were of particular interest, especially ones that required transfers of large amounts of foreign exchange abroad or that relied heavily on debt financing originating in the home market. Although HNA and Wanda survived the scrutiny, albeit with changed behaviour, Anbang was a casualty for reasons discussed below, and the enterprise was dissolved.

MAJOR CHINESE MERGERS AND ACQUISITIONS IN 2016

When Chinese entities began investing abroad in the 1980s, the initial objective was, as noted, to source natural resources and later to acquire producers in the developing world. Acquisitions in Europe and North America followed after the turn of the century. Most of these were small deals, but there were two large exceptions in the Canadian energy industry by Chinese SOEs: in 2010 Sinopec paid $4.6 billion for a share of Canada's Syncrude, and in 2013 CNOOC acquired Nexen, an oil and gas company, in a $15 billion acquisition.

The capital surge that took place in 2016 included ten deals individually valued at more than $3 billion, listed in Table 4.1 and summarized below.[4] Together they illustrate the diversity of investors and their sectoral targets. All but one investor was a privately owned enterprise or a hybrid in which ownership was unclear. US firms were targets in six of the ten acquisitions. As for their sectoral targets, entertainment and tourism dominated with five deals. Wanda, HNA, and Anbang became the focus of an official crackdown, however, on the grounds that their entertainment and tourism deals were not in the national interest.

Anbang Insurance Group: This company was founded in 2004 as an auto insurer, but quickly branched into asset management and became one of China's largest insurance companies, with an estimated $114 billion in assets. In June 2017, however, Anbang's chairman and founder was relieved of his responsibilities and in May 2018 sentenced to eighteen years in jail on fraud and embezzlement charges. Presumably because of these convictions, which reportedly are under appeal, in June 2018 nearly all of Anbang's assets were transferred to the China Insurance Security Fund while the state sought a private buyer.

Anbang's fall from grace followed a series of widely publicized international acquisitions in South Korea, the Netherlands, Belgium,

Table 4.1 Top Ten Mergers and Acquisitions by Chinese Firms, 2016

Date of Deal	Acquirer	Acquired	Value ($ billions)	Sector	Ownership of Acquirer
January	Dalian Wanda	Legendary Entertainment (US)	3.5	entertainment	private
January	Haier	GE Appliances (US)	5.4	consumer	private
January	China-Three Gorges	Duke Energy (Brazil)	3.7	energy	state
February	HNA	Ingram Micro (US)	6.0	electronics distribution	hybrid
March	Anbang	Strategic Hotels (US)	5.7	tourism	private
April	Apex Technology	Lexmark (US)	3.6	technology	private
June	Tencent	Supercell (Finland)	8.6	entertainment	private
August	Shanghai Giant Consortium	Playtika (Israel)	4.4	entertainment	private
August	Midea	Kuka (EU)	4.7	technology/ robotics	private
October	HNA	Hilton Hotels (25%) (US)	6.5	tourism	hybrid
TOTAL			51.9		

Source: Yang Ying, "China's top ten global M&A deals in 2016," *China Daily*, 1 June 2017, available online at http://www.chinadaily.com.cn/bizchina/2017top10/ 2017-06/01/content_29568764.htm.

the United Kingdom, and the United States. Two US acquisitions were particularly high profile: the Waldorf Astoria Hotel in 2014 and a large share of Strategic Hotels and Resorts in 2016. A bid for Starwood hotels in 2016 was withdrawn, however, under pressure from Chinese financial regulators concerned about managing the risks of a large acquisition in an industry outside Anbang's core competence in insurance.

Chinese insurers face a dilemma: their customer base is aging, and therefore their liabilities from insuring these customers are rising at the same time that asset growth is slowing in the home market. One way to resolve this dilemma is to acquire foreign-income-generating assets. Anbang's approach was to grow its income in China by selling universal life policies – risky wealth-management products promising high returns in a short period but that contrast sharply with the longer-term, protection-focused policies offered by the industry both inside and outside China. Anbang also diversified beyond foreign insurance assets into real estate and hotels as it sought to escape the increasingly tightly regulated home market by moving capital abroad. Regulators reacted negatively to the evidence of this capital movement, especially into risky foreign real estate and hotels deemed to be outside Anbang's core competence. In December 2016 the State Administration of Foreign Exchange moved to block acquisitions judged to be speculative, while permitting "strategic" acquisitions or ones with synergies with the acquirer's domestic business in China.[5] In May 2017 Anbang was suspended from issuing new products for three months because of its apparent tolerance of high risks in these products, which "deviate from the fundamentals of insurance."

Dalian Wanda Group: This company was also singled out by concerned regulators, who focused on six of its recent foreign acquisitions. They restricted Wanda's assets, directing banks to stop funding the acquisitions and to refuse any proposal by Wanda to use offshore assets as collateral for other financing. Regualtors also prohibited Wanda from injecting cash from its domestic businesses into offshore ones.

Wanda was founded in 1988 as a private company. It became active in commercial real estate – claiming to have developed its commercial properties into the world's largest real estate enterprise – and aggressively expanded its Cultural Industries Group into China's largest cultural enterprise. In 2015 the Dalian Wanda Group reported assets of $44 billion.[6] Since 2009 the group has also pursued a number of international acquisitions in sports marketing and real estate, with deals in the United Kingdom and elsewhere in Europe. Those best known, however, are in entertainment, with high-profile US acquisitions that included AMC Entertainment, one of the world's largest theatre operators, in 2012 and Legendary Entertainment in 2016. Regulators, however, labelling these as a "buying spree," moved in July 2017 to restrict bank funding for further international acquisitions by Wanda or for transfers to its offshore subsidiaries. Wanda responded by selling a portfolio of tourism and hotel projects in China to a Chinese holding company and refocusing on its core real estate business model.[7]

HNA Group: In mid-2017 this company was subjected to intense scrutiny since, like Wanda, it had been on a "buying spree," acquiring tourism and other assets valued at $40 billion over a twenty-eight-month period.[8] By some estimates, HNA – a privately held conglomerate that has leveraged existing assets to fund the purchase of new ones – is one of China's most aggressive deal makers.[9] HNA was founded in 2000 as Hainan Airlines, which remains its flagship unit, and a local airfreight company on the island of Hainan. At its height HNA Group had as many as one hundred and eighty thousand employees worldwide. In 2015 it became a Fortune 500 company reporting $90 billion in assets. Its divisions include aviation, tourism, shipping, retail, real estate, and financial services. Its international assets have included New Zealand's largest financial services firm, a stake in Hilton Worldwide, aviation service companies in fourteen countries, and a large shareholding in Deutsche Bank (before reducing its stake twice, in 2018 and 2019). HNA's acquisition spree included thirty-five deals worth an estimated $27 billion. The 25 per cent stake in Hilton Worldwide was divested in early 2018 as changes in financial regulation in China reduced the possibility of rolling over debts in regulators' quest to reduce leverage in large conglomerates such as HNA.

Unlike its real estate assets, however, HNA's acquisition in 2016 of Ingram Micro, an electronics products distributor, was seen to strengthen its capabilities, in this case through the use of Ingram's supply chain network. Ingram's international profile was seen as a positive factor in the expansion of HNA's foothold in emerging market economies. Since this transaction was also the largest-ever Chinese takeover of an American IT company, the deal was reviewed by US regulators on security grounds and subsequently approved. As with Anbang and Wanda, Chinese regulators scrutinized the transaction in June 2017 for its potential to contribute to systemic financial risk. Unlike with the other two, however, there are few signs of similar bank lending restrictions on HNA Group. Company spokespeople have defended its acquisitions as part of a disciplined strategy,[10] yet in late 2018 HNA moved to sell Ingram as it sought to reduce its indebtedness.

Apex Technology: In contrast to the three preceding troubled companies, Apex Technology's acquisition of Lexmark was quite straightforward. Founded in 2000 in Zhuhai, Guangdong province, Apex designs, manufactures, and markets inkjet and laser cartridge components and other core printer parts. It is one of the world's largest manufacturers of global aftermarket imaging supplies and cartridge chips, marketed through a sales network that extends to more than a hundred countries. Apex is listed on the Shenzhen Stock Exchange, with nearly 70 per cent of its shares held by Zhuhai Seine Technology. The Lexmark acquisition was a transaction that relates directly to Apex's core business in the acquisition of a global brand, and with it, enlarged its market share, described by the company as a means to "build a global printer empire" and as a "landmark event for the global printing industry."[11]

Haier: This company is well known for its successful emergence from modest origins as the collectively owned Qingdao Refrigerator Factory. With the company facing bankruptcy in 1984, its founder and chief executive officer, Ruimin Zhang, began its transformation into a global home appliance brand. He succeeded in transforming

Haier from an imitator into a world-famous innovative company by constantly adjusting business strategies to the demands of the market environment. Haier internationalized by positioning itself as a local brand in various markets, rather than by acquiring local assets. It is now a multinational with more than sixty thousand employees, distributing its products in some twenty-five countries. In 2013 Haier was selected as Forbes Asia's "Fabulous Fifty" company. In 1993 Haier listed a subsidiary, Qingdao Haier Refrigerators, on the Shanghai Stock Exchange, and in 2005 acquired a controlling stake in Haier CCT Holding, a publicly listed joint venture on the Hong Kong Stock Exchange.

With the acquisition of GE Appliances, Zhang is reportedly moving to transform Haier from a manufacturer into a distributor of consumer goods and services, including food delivery via the Internet. The aim is to become a networked company of independent business units that act like customer-focused startups. GE Appliances will be given considerable autonomy with respect to its future strategy and business development. For Haier this is a market-seeking transaction; for GE it is the successful exit of its North American brand manufacturing business, which had been on the market for some time. Haier sees the GE brand as a way to expand its market share while leveraging the brand with Haier's innovative capabilities.

GD Midea Group: Midea was founded in 1968 in Beijiao, Guangdong province, to produce plastic parts. It then expanded into the production of electric fans and appliances, and in 1993 was listed as a public company on the Shenzhen Stock Exchange. It is now both a Fortune 500 company and a Fortune Global 2000 company. It is also China's biggest appliance manufacturer and a close competitor to Haier as beneficiary of a government subsidy to rural residents to enable them to purchase modern appliances. Midea still leads Haier in retail sales volume, but this has been declining in recent years.

In 2016 Midea attracted international attention with its acquisition of nearly 50 per cent of German robot maker Kuka AG. Unlike some other transactions, this one was not about acquiring brand or an international presence. Rather, the purchase of the German company represented the acquisition of technical capabilities to apply to Midea's existing China-based operations. Midea has said its goal is to transform its manufacturing with robot technology (it already uses Kuka robots in its factories), allowing it to reduce its workforce by 20 per cent by 2018. In 2014 smartphone maker Xiaomi took a 1.3 per cent stake in Midea with the intention of applying smart phones to home-appliance operations.

Tencent Holdings: This company, founded in 1998, describes itself as "an Internet Technology and Cultural Enterprise." It is a leading provider of Internet value-added services in China, and has been listed on the Hong Kong Stock Exchange since 2004. Tencent provides social platforms and digital-content services through communications, information, entertainment, and financial services.[12] By 2017 its computer gaming business was growing at an 11 per cent annual rate with the introduction of popular new games and eSports. Online gaming revenue grew by 28 per cent in 2017, and Tencent's share of the Chinese online payments market was more than 39 per cent, second only to Alipay's. In late 2017 Tencent's market capitalization topped US$500 billion.[13]

Tencent emphasizes development and innovation capabilities, with more than half of its employees designated as R&D staff. Tencent Research Institute was set up in 2007 with a 100 million renminbi investment in campuses in Beijing, Shanghai, and Shenzhen. The acquisition in 2016 of a majority stake in Supercell, a mobile game maker, for an estimated $8.6 billion expanded Tencent's capabilities by adding a globally recognized innovator to its global games network. The acquisition of Supercell, whose games are played by one hundred million people daily, is intended to develop games for the global market. Supercell will maintain its base in Finland and contribute its production model of working in small independent teams or "cells" to the enterprise.

Implications of the 2016 Outward FDI Surge

The above cases illustrate both domestic and international drivers of business decisions to invest abroad. Investors seek new markets through trade and by the acquisition of new or better technologies, product brands, and better distribution networks. Escaping regulatory restrictions in the home market is also a common motivation. In the ten transactions listed in Table 4.1, three of the investors – Apex Technology, Haier, and HNA Group – sought to expand their global market share, while Tencent's aim was to develop a global market presence with the Supercell acquisition. Brand seeking was also an evident driver in Apex Technology's acquisition of Lexmark, a well-known global brand. Haier's improvement strategy was also successfully leveraged into a brand, while Tencent deliberately sought a global brand that could be used to establish a more prominent presence in international markets – and to encourage innovation in existing operations. Relatedly, the Tencent acquisition and HNA Group's hotel and tourism acquisitions aimed to expand core capabilities. Midea is the sole example of a transaction undertaken primarily to learn and use acquired technology to expand its core capabilities in its domestic operations, rather than abroad.

The three sizable enterprises that attracted regulatory attention and penalties aspired to enlarge their presence in international markets, but they were using financing strategies that regulators regarded as contributing to systemic risk in China. Anbang's strategy was also designed to escape domestic financial regulatory restrictions by using foreign capital to diversify the term structure of its financial assets. Significantly, within three years, all three companies had unwound some or all of their foreign acquisitions.

These cases offer useful insights into larger policy trends in China. Chinese policy and regulatory frameworks had a significant influence on enterprise behaviour by encouraging firms to "go out." With the shift in policy focus to rebalancing and restructuring the economy, the state-owned banks also changed firms' behaviour through their willingness to accommodate domestic corporate borrowing, ostensibly to support real economic growth. This emphasis on debt-financed growth had consequences both intended and unintended, as evident in the three prominent cases where bank oversight of the actual uses of these funds appears to have been inadequate, as domestic funds were used to finance foreign acquisitions. In retrospect, however, it is apparent that acquisitions of foreign assets peaked in 2016 as regulators insisted that large foreign transactions be consistent with core businesses. SOE ChemChina's acquisition of Swiss-based Syngenta for $43 billion, completed in June 2017, although a large transaction, was clearly one that would expand ChemChina's core competence and bring valuable knowledge assets into the Chinese economy. Permitted transactions will still be funded by Chinese financial institutions, but there will be increased regulatory sensitivity to significant capital outflows and their exchange-rate effects.

Finally it should be noted that the lag in official recognition of the consequences of increased corporate leverage was partly due to the underdeveloped state of coordination among financial regulators and the central bank, and institutions such as the National Development and Reform Commission and the Ministry of Commerce that are responsible for outward FDI policy. When the authorities recognized the potential systemic risks in late 2016, they increased regulatory scrutiny of acquirers' proposed transactions and imposed capital controls to reduce pressures on the use of foreign exchange reserves to prevent unwanted exchange-rate depreciation. These measures were the main reason the investment boom ended. Thirty potential acquisitions of US and European assets valued at $75 billion were cancelled in 2016, including Anbang's proposed acquisition of Starwood Hotels & Resorts.[14] The effects of the changed policy environment are evident in the list of major transactions in 2017 in Table 4.2.

Table 4.2 Top Ten Mergers and Acquisitions by Chinese Firms, 2017

Date of Deal	Acquirer	Acquired	Value ($ billions)	Sector	Ownership of Acquirer
July	Vanke, Hopu, SMG … Bank of China	GLP (Singapore)	16.1	real estate	private
June	China Investment Corp	Logicor Europe (UK)	13.8	real estate	sovereign wealth fund
July	COSCO Shipping	Orient Overseas (HK)	8.4	transportation	state
September	Shanghai Energy Fund	Rosneft (Russia)*	9.0	oil & gas	private
January	State Grid Corp of China	CPFL Energia (Brazil)	3.5	utility & energy	state
January	Yankuang	Coal & Allied Industries (Australia)	3.1	mining	state
July	Didi Chuxing, SoftBank, and others	Grab (Singapore)	2.5	technology	private
August	Bohai Capital	Hong Kong Aviation (Hong Kong)	2.3	finance/aircraft leasing	private
September	State Power Investment	Power Station (Brazil)	2.3	utility & energy	state
January	Ant Financial	MoneyGram (US)**	2.0	finance	private
TOTAL			63.1		

* Transaction delayed, March 2018.
** Acquisition abandoned, January 2018.
Source: Pan Yue, "2017 in Review: China's Top 10 Outbound Deals Reflect Beijing Crackdown on 'Unsound' Investment," *China Money Network*, 8 December 2017, available online at https://www.chinamoneynetwork.com/2017/12/08/2017-review-chinas-overseas-investment-remains-robust-140b-despite-tight-regulations.

CHINESE OUTWARD FDI IN 2017

A comparison of Tables 4.1 and 4.2 reveals marked differences in Chinese outward FDI in 2016 and 2017, with significant implications. In 2016 most of the acquired firms were American, with Chinese acquirers in the entertainment, tourism, and consumer products businesses (six of ten) and the remainder in technology and energy. In addition, most of the Chinese acquirers were privately owned enterprises. Three transactions in hotels and entertainment were unwound in response to regulatory pressures.

As Table 4.2 shows, major transactions reported in 2017 contrasted in several dimensions from those in 2016. Only one target firm on the list was American; the others were in Asia and the Pacific (including Australia), Brazil (2), the United Kingdom, and Russia (one each). It should be noted that the Bohai Capital acquisition was part of a larger set of transactions during that period, when Bohai Leasing, controlled by HNA, acquired Avolon Holdings, an aircraft leasing company owned by HNA, which in turn acquired the aircraft leasing unit of CIT Group, a US financial services holding company, for $10 billion.

Of the ten transactions, SOEs and China's sovereign wealth fund accounted for five, while three of the five private acquirers were large equity players. The sectoral composition of these transactions showed a marked change from a year earlier, with the majority directly related to natural resources and related acquisitions. Four were in energy and utilities and mining, four in transportation and logistics, and two in technology. MoneyGram, the US acquisition, was abandoned in the face of regulatory pressures from the CFIUS. The bidder for Rosneft encountered both financial troubles and regulatory pressures that continued to delay completion into 2018.

Two main factors help explain the changes in sectoral composition of transactions over the two years. First, Chinese policy towards capital outflows was significantly tightened in late 2016 as the size of capital outflows "melted away" China's foreign-exchange reserves and as policy placed more weight on the potential value of the proposed investments to China's long-term development objectives. The second factor was changes in host-country policies towards the review and approval of outward FDI transactions. In the United States, where China is now seen as a strategic rival, there are increased political pressures for more stringent criteria to evaluate the implications of acquisitions of technology, evident in Ant Financial's abandoned bid for MoneyGram.

Those sectors experiencing the largest declines in transactions were entertainment, consumer products and services, and real estate and hospitality – sectors deemed to have dubious value to national development. Less evident is the diversification into other sectors, such as health, biotech, IT, transportation, and infrastructure, that experienced stable investment and growth. Most acquisitions of US assets in 2017 were by privately owned enterprises, although SOEs were responsible for three deals in energy and mining.[15]

Changes in policies were the main driver of these sectoral and other developments. Tighter regulatory controls were placed on outward FDI by directing banks to limit the conversion of renminbi into foreign currency for foreign acquisitions and by informally blocking foreign investments that might cause large capital outflows. A new outward FDI management regime was also created that classifies sectors as encouraged, restricted, or prohibited. "Encouraged" firms include BRI-related infrastructure, investments that promote competitiveness in export markets and Chinese technical standards outside China, high-tech and advanced manufacturing investments, oil and gas, energy and mining, and agricultural and services sector investments. The "restricted" category includes real estate, entertainment, hospitality – the "guilty" sectors in 2016 – and financial investments unrelated to physical projects abroad. The "prohibited" sectors include businesses exporting unapproved core technologies, those prohibited by international agreements, or those that could harm China's interests and security.[16]

A mid-year summary by New York-based Rhodium Group of the effects of this tighter regulatory oversight shows that new activity dropped by 20 per cent in the first quarter of 2017, but recovered somewhat in the second quarter.[17] Moreover, large transactions comparable to those in 2016 were not repeated, and the declining size of the deals was then reflected in reduced capital outflows.

THE FUTURE OF CHINESE CAPITAL: UNCERTAINTY, OPPORTUNITY, AND RISK

By 2018 the slowing pace of new activity added to growing uncertainty about future trends in Chinese outward FDI.[18] Rhodium Group's 2018 summary estimates a drop of 84 per cent from a year earlier in the number of Chinese companies completing acquisitions and greenfield investments. In 2016 completed Chinese investment in the United States totalled $46 billion, fell to $29 billion in 2017, and in 2018 hit a seven-year low of $4.8 billion.[19] Adding to Beijing's crackdown on outward investment is increasing US regulatory scrutiny of Chinese acquisitions in the United States. Chinese private investors are now constrained at home by capital controls and tighter financial conditions that, among other things, limit debt rollovers, which had become a common practice. At the same time, US regulatory hurdles have increased the time and costs of completing transactions; indeed, HNA, Wanda, and Anbang are now selling US assets. Rhodium Group also notes the marked shift in sectoral composition towards investments in health and biotech. By mid-year 2018, Chinese venture capital investment in US biotech companies totalled $5.1 billion, surpassing the $4 billion record total for the entire year in 2017.[20] Beijing's new focus on medicine – cancer research, in particular – as a strategic sector had not yet attracted the attention of US regulators.[21] The numbers of investments in hotels, real estate, and entertainment are still significant, but they are much smaller and do not cause capital outflows.

The policy trend is now clear but its trajectory is uncertain. China-US trade tensions and fears of a trade war reflect a heightened rivalry between the two superpowers touched off by two main factors. One is President Xi Jinping's widely publicized ambitious goals for MIC 2025 to make China a world leader in advanced manufacturing, and his global connectedness vision for the Belt and Road Initiative. The other factor is the Trump administration's increased focus on Chinese acquisitions of US technology, allegedly by unfair means, which the administration insists must stop. Tariffs are its weapon of choice, particularly the unilateral application of US Section 301 tariffs (on its trading partners, not just China) on a widening range of goods and the use of tariffs for national security reasons under Section 232 (b) of the Trade Expansion Act.

The effect of these US policies on Chinese outward FDI is likely to be negative. Tighter policies will increase transactions costs by widening the scope and processes of security screenings by the CFIUS and defining them in the Foreign Investment Risk Review Modernization Act. The US Department of Commerce is also being directed to impose stricter controls on technology transfers to foreign firms. These measures are discouraging Chinese FDI that might develop R&D facilities that have security or military applications, such as machine learning and semiconductors. Additional restrictions also might be forthcoming as outcomes of Section 301 investigations.

Although these developments imply growing restrictions on cross-border FDI to and from China, the underlying assumption – that China engages in forced technology transfers – should be evaluated against the statistical evidence. Missing from the popular narrative is evidence that China's protection of intellectual property is improving. Nicholas Lardy has pointed out that China's payments of licensing fees and royalties for using foreign technology nearly tripled between 2007 and 2017, and according to the IMF China ranks fourth in the world in the size of its annual payments to acquire technology.[22] As well, the Canada-China Business Council reports that, in 2016, concerns about Chinese infringements of their intellectual property were of declining importance to Canadian businesses.[23]

The negative US stance also might create incentives for foreign manufacturers to localize production behind the US tariff wall. The European Union and other economies will continue to seek Chinese capital and business to offset their slow growth prospects. Host markets also stand to benefit as Chinese firms build channels in their value chains for foreign suppliers to access the Chinese market – access that could be useful to small firms in Western markets. In sectors such as e-commerce, electronics, machinery, environmental technology, and transportation infrastructure, Chinese firms are among the world's largest and most advanced. Infrastructure firms, for instance, could provide channels for engineering and design firms to become suppliers to the BRI, which, among other things, seeks to facilitate adjustments by China's old industrial sectors, such as iron and steel, by channelling excess capacity into infrastructure projects in underserved markets in neighbouring countries.

Given the potential opportunities, many host countries will continue to seek Chinese capital, including cross-border mergers and acquisitions, much of which will create benefits for world consumers as well as providing technological advances, price competition, and business innovation. Risks exist, however, that have policy implications.

FUTURE ISSUES: SYSTEM DIFFERENCES AND TECHNOLOGY

One key policy implication is that China is becoming a major global source of capital, a trend that will continue but perhaps shift in direction to countries other than the United States. Estimates of the magnitude of China's outward flows illustrate this point. According to United Nations statistics, in 2017 China's global stock of outward FDI was $1.48 trillion – the US total was $7.8 trillion – up from just $27 billion in 1999 and equivalent to 12 per cent of China's GDP.[24] If China's GDP growth were to continue at 6 per cent annual rates and the ratio between outward FDI and GDP remained 12 per cent, by 2020 the total stock of Chinese outward FDI would be more than $1.7 trillion, a 13 per cent increase over 2017. The total might be even larger if the domestic economy grows more slowly and outward investment picks up in search of more global opportunities. Either way, the numbers are large.

Second, host governments that seek to minimize the risks of Chinese mergers and acquisitions while remaining open to the benefits of cross-border investment face substantial differences between the Chinese system and their own, as I recount in Canada's case in the final chapter. In general, many market participants and analysts argue that some key changes are desirable in China, beginning with a more transparent regime to govern outward FDI. Moves in this direction were announced by the State Council in November 2018, and were included in Chinese commitments in China-US trade and technology talks in early 2019. Achieving this greater transparency, however, would require more robust regulatory capacities to enforce policies and ensure they have the desired effect on investor behaviour.

Political and policy differences also appear in commercial transactions, particularly those with Chinese SOEs, whose decisions might be driven by political, rather than commercial, criteria. This is a particular concern to Canadians. Separating government ownership from enterprise management is a challenge that could be addressed by introducing modern corporate governance practices and applying more stringent transparency requirements to SOEs. Although accounting and external audit practices are gradually becoming more independent, the pace is slow. Financial investors also might have objectives that conflict with national policy objectives – evident in Chinese regulators' concerns about firms using mergers and acquisitions as a form of capital flight, as hedges against currency devaluation, or in response to the anti-corruption campaign.

Host governments nevertheless should remain open to the net benefits of Chinese investment. Until recently there were relatively few barriers to Chinese FDI in North America or western Europe. Since 1975 the United States has relied on the CFIUS to screen proposed acquisitions for national security concerns. Screening has been reasonably light handed, and few deals have been formally blocked. But rising geopolitical tensions and rivalry are changing this behaviour as the US administration imposes tariffs on a widening range of Chinese goods and China retaliates. Some, perhaps many, Chinese firms are likely to look for alternative investment locations such as Canada and Europe, while adding to the Chinese presence in Africa, Latin America, and eastern Europe.

Canada, too, has a record of accepting Chinese mergers and acquisitions, with ninety-seven deals completed between 1996 and 2015 – again, mostly small, with only six having reported values of more than $1 billion. Despite this apparent openness, however, in the past decade the OECD has rated Canada as having an opaque FDI screening system, requiring security screening, a "net benefits" test, and, since December 2012, a restriction on SOEs owning controlling stakes in oil sands companies other than in unspecified "exceptional circumstances." Canadian authorities have blocked few deals, although the rejection of a hostile bid for Potash Corporation by BHP Billiton of Australia in 2012 was highly visible.[25] The current federal government has signalled its desire to attract Chinese capital to aid its growth objectives, but has made few changes to address the OECD's criticisms of the opaque screening regime.

Western Europe has also been relatively open to Chinese investment, with 362 completed deals between 1988 and 2015, twenty-one of which had reported values greater than $1 billion. Some countries do not have an investment screening regime. It is not clear whether current pressures arising from lagging economies, immigration debates, and Brexit negotiations risk creating barriers, but European and Chinese leaders recognize each other's economies as significant partners through trade and capital flows. Recognition of the risks we outlined earlier suggest the need for a clearer framework for the European relationship by negotiating bilateral investment agreements or developing a joint dialogue with both the United States and Canada on the elusive goal of global governance for investment, which inevitably must include China.

The third implication is growing political concern about China's pursuit of high-tech deals. Already there is a backlash in Europe in the wake of bids by Chinese firms seeking to leapfrog competitors by acquiring advanced technology – Midea's quest for Kuka, discussed earlier, is an example – and it is a significant concern in US debates about reciprocity and openness to international trade. These concerns have implications for industry competition, technological development, and national security. The core challenges are respect for and enforcement of intellectual property rights, non-discrimination, and reciprocity in market access. Chinese firms are developing technical skills by learning from their Western competitors through the purchase of technologies and through acquisitions. Yet foreign firms in China continue to report requirements for quotas and local content, denial of market access, and discriminatory industrial policies to force technology sharing. This lack of reciprocity is becoming a powerful factor in the growing US sense of unfairness concerning China-US trade, which the current administration is using to justify labelling China a strategic rival.

CONCLUSION

China's new era of capital and competition has attracted an increasingly intense US backlash in response to China's stated technology ambitions and unfair policies and practices to acquire foreign technologies. Backlash is not limited to America: charges of unfair business practices have been levelled at China's state-owned financial institutions for their lending practices in Malaysia, Pakistan, India, and Myanmar.

Although the long-standing objective to "go out" remains, China's outward investment boom peaked in 2016 because of problems at home, negative effects on the domestic economy, and revealed weaknesses in China's regulatory frameworks. The top ten investments in 2017 indicate a changing composition of investors and acquisitions as Chinese corporate decision makers wrestle with the effects of the country's slowing growth and declining returns on investors' domestic assets. These are reasons to expect the pace of Chinese outward FDI to continue to slow. At the same time, the United States' dramatic expansion of export controls on sensitive technologies and increasingly restrictive approach to approvals of new transactions mean that Chinese outward FDI flows are likely to be directed to countries in Europe, Africa, and those along the Belt and Road, the initiative to which I turn next.

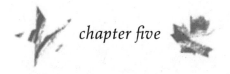

chapter five

THE BELT AND ROAD INITIATIVE: CHINA REACHES OUT

When President Xi Jinping launched the westward-leading One Belt, One Road initiative in 2013 to connect China with its Eurasian neighbours, he described it as the modern version of the ancient Silk Road, a global public good widely accessible to all. As the project evolved, it was renamed the Belt and Road Initiative for its proposed maritime (Belt) and land (Road) routes that would connect more than sixty-five countries estimated to account for a third of global GDP and two-thirds of the total population (Figure 5.1).[1] These are countries desperate to improve their infrastructure to increase their long-term growth potential. Estimates of total investments over the life of the project vary between $1 trillion and $8 trillion.[2]

In its first five years, what began as a regional infrastructure initiative became a prominent feature of Xi's long game to expand China's global presence. There are many different views of the BRI's potential, but it has variously been called the latest phase in the rationalization and expansion of China's earlier reform and opening up,[3] the "largest overseas investment drive ever launched by a single country,"[4] and as "the project of the century," with potentially game-changing implications for China's global influence and for the balance of power.

The BRI has also had bad headlines, however, including about practices of "debt trap diplomacy" and the initiative's being a new

Figure 5.1 The Belt and Road Initiative

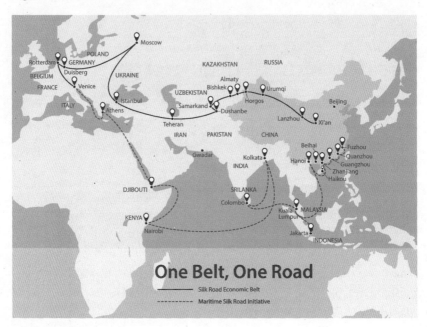

Source: iStock.com/hakule.

form of colonialism. Financial flows in the initial phase of the BRI have been dominated by bank loans channelled to neighbouring countries and to resource-rich developing economies. Some argue that these flows, along with development aid and financial support, are intended to support China's goal of becoming a leading member of the international community by encouraging other countries to enter its system of rules.[5] But Australian strategic studies expert Hugh White argues China's motive is to consolidate its position at the centre of global supply chains and manufacturing networks. To that end, the BRI provides an opportunity to develop technologies and set standards that will have global significance as China consolidates its position as an upper-middle-income country.[6] Still others argue that the BRI is a way to deploy China's excess industrial capacity and production to its less-developed neighbours. Jin Liqun, founding president of the Asian Infrastructure Investment Bank (AIIB) founded by China, counters that, although the initiative has attracted attention to China's own interests, its central purpose is to promote connectivity and economic integration as a public good accessible to all by investing in badly needed infrastructure projects across Asia, into Europe, Africa, and, more recently, Latin America.

In May 2017, President Xi chaired the inaugural Belt and Road Forum in Beijing, attended by twenty-nine heads of state and delegates from more than one hundred countries. The Forum celebrated the creation in 2015 of the Asian Infrastructure Investment Bank with US$100 billion in initial capital that sets the rules, but ones that are very much in line with international norms. China is also cooperating with the other so-called BRICs group of developing economies – Brazil, Russia, India, and China – to create a New Development Bank to mobilize resources for development projects.[7]

Although Chinese leaders' objectives for the BRI sound grandiose, even visionary, the challenges lie in implementation. In its first half-decade, the BRI's record is a mix of successes and significant problems, of learning about the inevitable weaknesses and major problems of infrastructure projects. Infrastructure megaprojects have a venerable history in both developed and developing countries of providing new facilities and connectivity, whether in post-conflict reconstruction, projects to update and modernize facilities, or projects for economic development. But large, long-term, cross-border infrastructure investment projects that appear politically attractive – indeed, the long-term benefits of well-planned, well-timed projects are substantial – are fraught with political and practical risks.

The BRI's reported sources of finance have relied heavily on debt finance through loans from China's policy banks and state-owned commercial banks. A review of high-profile problem cases leads to the conclusion that much work is needed to standardize governance procedures and lending standards among this plethora of lending institutions. Institutional reforms could also help to diffuse project risks. In the absence of such change, there are many reports of political backlash generated by Chinese interests, policies, and business practices. Continuing these practices could undermine both China's reputation and the BRI's future prospects, and have undesirable geopolitical effects in the light of the US decision to brand China as a strategic competitor.

THE BRI'S MISSION AND PERFORMANCE SINCE 2014

The BRI has both international and domestic objectives. At the local level, Chinese authorities see the BRI as a way to develop connections between youthful populations in neighbouring countries and the aging Chinese population and China's shrinking labour force. BRI megaprojects also might be of a scale that allows China to redirect excess production by industrial SOEs – such as steel and cement makers – to new markets where demand is growing. Developing new markets, in turn, could open opportunities to shift the composition of Chinese exports from consumer goods produced by the "world's workshop" to higher-value-added capital goods. For example, telecom equipment, construction machinery, and turbines will all be in demand as the economy restructures to produce more services in construction and engineering and to realize China's goal to lead in advanced manufacturing.

In 2017 the Fitch ratings agency reported that BRI projects worth US$900 billion were either planned or under way.[8] Since then the results and implications have begun to appear. A wave of fundraising and institution building since 2014 has created a number of prominent infrastructure projects. A centrepiece is the China-Pakistan Economic Corridor (CPEC), which runs from the Chinese border through Pakistan to the port of Gwadar on the Arabian Sea. Other major projects include construction of an oil pipeline through Myanmar to Yunnan province, and development of the Greek port of Piraeus into a transshipment hub for trade between Asia and Europe. China's tech giants are also engaging with the BRI as Alibaba and Ant Financial invest in Bangladesh and develop mobile payment and digital financial services in Pakistan through a strategic partnership.

Chinese financial institutions have allocated significant funding to the BRI. In 2014 China's sovereign wealth fund created a Silk Road Fund of $40 billion. The *Financial Times* has reported that, by the end of 2014, two major Chinese policy banks had made loans of nearly $700 billion,[9] while in 2015 $82 billion was transferred by the Chinese state to three state-owned banks to fund BRI projects.[10] By the end of 2017, the AIIB had approved twenty-three projects and invested $4.2 billion; projects tended to cluster in the energy sector (ten) and in transportation (six) as a variety of infrastructure projects got under way in thirteen countries: Azerbaijan (1), Bangladesh (2), Georgia (1), India (5), Indonesia (3), Myanmar (1), Oman (2), Pakistan (2), the Philippines (1), and Tajikistan (2).[11] Information on the cost of funds is scarce, but available data show that the majority of these projects were financed by loans. The Chinese Ministry of Commerce reports that the Silk Road Fund had invested US$6 billion in fifteen projects, while the China Development Bank had issued US$168 billion in loans, and loan commitments by the Export-Import Bank of China totalled more than US$101 billion. Three state-owned commercial banks had also provided credit.

Some estimates of the potential effects of the BRI on trade and investment flows in the region and on actual and potential growth are available. The Economist Intelligence Unit estimates that, by the first quarter of 2018, most BRI trade and investment flows were accounted for by ten countries, with Vietnam, Malaysia, Indonesia, Thailand, Singapore, and Russia in the lead – understandably, since project development in these economies would be easier than in less developed ones. Pakistan's significance is largely determined by the transportation potential of the CPEC.[12]

The Ministry of Commerce also reported in May 2018 that trade deals had risen by 19.2 per cent, year over year, in the first quarter of that year, while non-financial investment grew by 17.3 per cent. Free trade negotiations were reported to be under way with three countries, including Pakistan, and seventy-five economic and trade cooperation zones were being created with BRI countries.[13] A May 2017 report from the state-owned Assets Supervision and Administration Commission of the State Council announced that forty-seven central government SOEs were then involved in 1,676 projects in BRI countries.[14]

In these projects, there is a noticeable focus on land-based infrastructure, while growth in trade and investment is slow. Although detailed data from English-language sources are sparse and many reported projects predate BRI, one indicator that reflects expanding economic potential and reduced trade costs is the increased transcontinental rail services that are beginning to replace costly and slow-moving ocean transportation. By the end of 2016, forty such services had appeared, connecting cities in China and Europe. Seventeen hundred freight trains travelled from China to Europe in 2016, double the traffic in 2015.[15]

In March 2019 the BRI reached a new phase in its mission when the Italian government became the first G7 country to endorse the initiative. Rome's reported objectives are twofold: to attract Chinese investments that will enable it to diversify beyond dependence on Brussels, and to sell "Make in Italy" in China. China's motives are more strategic: to attract Italy into a dependent relationship by offering needed investments in aging Italian ports, and to extend Xi Jinping's vision of the BRI as a platform connecting China and Europe. The European Commission, for its part, has adopted a view similar to that of the United States, branding China a "systemic rival" that treats European companies unfairly.[16]

Infrastructure Projects: Some Risky Cases

Balancing these developments are indicators of significant risks, particularly those of indebtedness as governments struggle with debt repayments to Chinese financial institutions. Sceptics focus on both the quantitative and qualitative characteristics of project management by Chinese institutions and ask whether the BRI is a development agency or a new form of colonialism.[17] Some large BRI projects have attracted particularly intense international criticism because of the practice by Chinese lenders of requiring compensation in the form of equity stakes when borrowers are unable to repay loans – instead of, for example, rescheduling or forgiving the debts. Some argue that Chinese financial institutions are self-interested and purposely resort to expensive debt financing to acquire key assets such as ports.[18] Others counter by arguing that host countries might have domestic problems they are unable to manage and that Chinese interest rates are quite reasonable. Five cases illustrate the risks some borrowers and lenders have faced.

The BRI Centrepiece: The China-Pakistan Economic Corridor

The China-Pakistan Economic Corridor has gained prominence as a BRI project both for its significant scale and location and because of rising concerns about Pakistan's apparent inability to service its Chinese debts. The CPEC also has geopolitical significance as a land corridor linking southwestern China and the Arabian Sea through Gwadar, a potential gateway due to its location near the Strait of Hormuz, through which a fifth of the world's oil passes. By agreement between China and Pakistan, 91 per cent of Gwadar's port revenues for the next forty years will go to the port's operator, Chinese Overseas Port Holding Company, and 9 per cent to the Pakistan government.

The CPEC is also the site of industrial development, energy, and infrastructure projects – including a highway, railway, and pipeline – expected to total an estimated $60 billion.[19] At least $33 billion is expected to be invested in energy projects, with China providing 80 per cent of the financing, reportedly at high interest rates.[20] The scale of Pakistan's public debt-to-GDP ratio – nearly 70 per cent in 2017 – has attracted IMF concerns about its ability to service that debt.[21] Already China has moved to halt funding for three infrastructure projects. Progress on the Gwadar port is also slow, with few new berths to attract cargo vessels beyond those bound for Chinese projects located in the immediate area.[22] In late 2018 Pakistan reduced the scale and cost of the Karachi-Peshawar railroad project.

Other Problem Cases

In 2016, Sri Lanka and China agreed to develop lands adjoining the port of Hambantota, already a $2 billion underperforming investment and one that other lenders had refused to fund. There was also stiff resistance from Sri Lankan workers to the proposed land acquisition for an adjoining industrial park, who complained it would become a Chinese settlement. When the Sri Lankan government found it impossible to service the existing debt, the newly elected president sought and received $1.1 billion debt relief in exchange for granting a ninety-nine-year lease to a Chinese bank holding company on 80 per cent of the port.[23] Reports of this development attracted international criticism of China's objectives, a subject of considerable sensitivity around a project in such close proximity to India. Added to general concern was the existence of a similar deal made in Greece in 2016, when a Chinese shipping company was permitted to acquire a 67 per cent stake in the Port of Piraeus. As a result, China was developing a reputation for practising "debt diplomacy" by agreeing to loan-financed projects that countries might be unable to repay, which would affect their public finances and undermine their ownership of infrastructure assets.[24]

In another case, an investment by CITIC, a state-owned Chinese financial institution, in Kyaukpyu Port in Myanmar drew international criticism of its estimated $7.5 billion price tag as unnecessarily expensive, and raised questions about the risks of future debt distress and the strategically important port's falling into Chinese hands.[25] A more recent case with a high public profile is in Malaysia, where the costs of "unequal treaties" between Chinese SOEs and Malaysian interests for Chinese projects on the drawing board became a subject in that country's May 2018 general election. Projects valued at $23 billion were suspended, including the $20 billion China-backed East Coast Rail Link, the BRI's single largest project, and three pipelines. After the election, President Mahathir Mohamad set out to renegotiate the terms of project financing and, even though construction had started, he temporarily cancelled the project in early 2019. Pushback from elsewhere in the region about this BRI "failure" might have been a factor in China's subsequent agreement to renegotiate the project for a more modest price. As Mahathir observed, "China doesn't conquer countries, but increases its influence."[26] His actions marked the first time an Asian government had pushed back against the BRI in such a public way.

Taken together, these cases raise questions about the professionalism of project finance decisions by lending institutions and accusations of "debt traps." One China scholar, a student of the ancient Silk Road, has noted a historical parallel between the terms for leasing the port of Hambantota to China and those of the China's Qing rulers in ceding Hong Kong to the British.[27]

RISK MANAGEMENT IN INFRASTRUCTURE PROJECTS

This partial litany of difficulties and shortcomings in some high-profile BRI projects, of which that in Pakistan is one of the largest, indicates the importance of risk management, project design, and project finance in unleashing the BRI's economic potential. The IMF, in its spring 2018 evaluation of Pakistan's economy, warned of the country's rising current account deficit (4.8 per cent of national income), fiscal deficit (in absolute terms soon to be the highest in history), and estimated foreign currency reserves that are less than required to finance ten weeks of imports. In July 2018, following his election as president, Imran Khan revealed that Pakistan was so deeply in debt that he would have to seek IMF support. In October 2018 he followed through with a formal request for a bailout.

TWR Advisory Group, a Washington-based consultancy, estimates that, overall, BRI projects worth $419 billion, or 32 per cent of BRI total lending, have encountered performance delays, public opposition, or national security controversies.[28] A detailed evaluation of the performance of BRI projects indicates the need for a strong focus on *debt sustainability* – the provision of debt financing of a size that a country can repay without incurring "debt distress." The Center for Global Development in Washington[29] found that twenty-three of sixty-eight countries eligible for BRI lending were vulnerable to debt distress, adding substantially to the risks – which will only be magnified by additional lending. In eight countries, any BRI financing would add to the risks of debt distress.[30] The Center for Global Development also reminds us that infrastructure is a critical engine of growth in developing economies, but that with debt financing the fuel for this engine is public borrowing and should therefore support productive investment. Too much debt can have significant negative effects: if a country's growth performance is insufficient or revenues are inadequate to cover debt-servicing costs, its government will encounter debt distress and need to reduce or restructure its debt or, at the extreme, to default.

Ideally such project risks are minimized by careful *project selection and risk sharing*. Only projects that are financially, economically, and politically viable should be selected. They should also be environmentally and socially sustainable. Once selected they should be managed, recognizing that the growth effects of different investments will differ. This means risks should be diversified and reduced by, among other measures, partnering with other lenders and investors. Investment decisions should be decided jointly with the host country, rather than unilaterally by the lender, and assistance should be made available to indebted countries to repay their loans. Better public relations are required, including transparency with the local media and host communities, and investing companies should train local labour forces and work with all stakeholders, rather than focusing on the party in power.[31]

Partnering with other lenders and investors is of particular relevance to the BRI, especially in the early days of AIIB-funded projects, when precedents are created. Chinese investors might believe they achieve "multiplier effects" by relying mainly on other Chinese financing sources instead of partnering with established multilateral lenders such as the Asian Development Bank and the World Bank. But such a China-first strategy has already had negative consequences, including the perception that China "hijacks" projects. Instead of helping to expand China's international influence, smaller countries might hedge by seeking closer relationships with other large countries. Quality controls in the AIIB are essential. The BRI's long-term vision will bear fruit only if investments are seen to be of value to people in the region and to provide payoffs to Chinese and other foreign investors.

In light of the BRI's focus on public investment in infrastructure, lessons on *project design* could be applied based on the extensive experience of multilateral development banks and other institutions. For example, infrastructure investments could be timed to counter severe cyclical downturns, such as that following the 2008–09 global financial crisis. Carefully chosen investments in real assets, combined with coordinated expansionary macroeconomic policy, could help offset the recessionary effects of lower demand, maintain consumption, and stimulate growth through capital spending.

Such spending would increase aggregate demand and supply, raise productivity, and generate future economic returns. Importantly, fiscal expansion of this kind has been most effective as part of a cooperative strategy among countries, rather than by one government's acting on its own. Such spending is also more likely to have the desired effect if applied to already-approved projects that are more likely to expand aggregate demand quickly.

Another lesson from past experience is that not all forms of infrastructure spending have the same growth effects. Energy, communications, and transportation investments facilitate economic activity; maintaining and renewing infrastructure stocks often provides higher returns than new investments. Location also matters, since investments in one place can have spillover effects to other locations, especially in urban areas. Efficient public investment can serve as a catalyst for growth by supporting or enabling the delivery of key public services and by connecting firms and citizens to economic opportunities.[32]

Note, however, that it is possible to overinvest in infrastructure. Avoiding this outcome requires careful testing of public finance decisions for their strategic importance – and ensuring such projects will generate positive returns. It has been shown that efficient public investment can double the growth effect over time; investment thus should go far beyond short-term stimulus to enhance both productivity and long-term growth prospects.

Two other factors to take into account in project design are, first, the importance of accompanying changes in structural policies to remove obstacles to growth or to free up growth processes; and, second, the need for high standards in lending decisions. The AIIB, in particular, should make high-quality and inclusive lending decisions, not convenient political ones. Achieving this objective would require the implementation of prudent lending standards and the working out of an agreed approach to handling debt distress. Indeed debt distress – its causes and management – is of particular concern as lending by China's policy banks ramps up. As noted earlier, the China Development Bank and the Export-Import Bank of China have already made large loans that will require repayments totalling nearly $700 billion – equal to the total lending of the World Bank and six regional development banks.[33] According to some reports, China might be running out of resources to support the BRI because very few projects are financed in renminbi, which make the BRI dependent on a limited supply of US dollars. This development alone might push China to co-finance projects with multilateral institutions.[34]

The absence in the BRI of standardized procedures for pricing assets and of procedures to follow with respect to distressed debt in the event of project failure has undermined China's reputation amid charges of "debt trap diplomacy." The Center for Global Development argues strongly for the adoption of the same or harmonized prudent lending standards by all international organizations. A similarly agreed approach to managing distressed debtors is also required. There is much to learn and apply in this regard from the experience of the OECD-based Paris Club, a well-respected multilateral institution founded in 1956 that coordinates sustainable solutions to the payment difficulties encountered by debtor countries.[35] The Center for Global Development recommends a revised Paris Club organization that would include China as an architect to update its collective approach. The Export-Import Bank of China alone has credit exposure of $90 billion, so there is a strong argument for revising the existing coordinating institution to include China.

The importance of these concerns are illustrated by examples in Southeast Asian countries, where China's lack of experience with investment projects leads project managers to choose to work instead with Japanese, European, and US institutions, even if initial Chinese bids are financially and politically attractive. A recent example is a high-profile Chinese bid to supply high-speed rail in Indonesia.[36] Japan had worked on a project proposal that was overtaken by one from China based on the bidder's record of building such projects in China and on its financial capacity. The Chinese bidder readily met Indonesian conditions, including omitting a state guarantee on the project loan, waiving the requirement of a budget contribution from the Indonesian government, accepting to enter into a joint venture with Indonesian partners who would receive majority control, and other production and job-creation promises. In 2015 the Chinese consortium won the project by accepting unusually high financial, operational, and political risks. The project then hit a wall: eighteen months after breaking ground, construction still had not begun. One reason was that Jakarta had encountered difficulties obtaining the land required for the rail line, indicating lack of planning and preparation. This is not an isolated case. China has developed an international reputation for producing high-speed trains, but managing in foreign markets is challenging because of Chinese firms' lack of planning and preparation and their inadequate understanding of local markets and institutions. As a result, while China's trade with Southeast Asia flourishes, its investment performance in the region is weak.

BACKLASH: MIXED MESSAGES AND BAD NEWS

This focus on the need for risk management might suggest that China's infrastructure diplomacy has backfired, with major reputational costs. Yet one of China's objectives is to win new friends. To increase the probability of achieving that objective, Chinese lenders should draw upon accumulated experience at the World Bank, the multilateral development banks, and national aid programs to "up their game" in terms of standards setting and debt sustainability.

Much can be done to reduce risk and improve future performance.[37] Multilateralizing the BRI is an obvious option, but potential partners might have reservations about the economic viability of the projects and less tolerance of high levels of corruption and other institutional weaknesses in borrowing countries. Also noted is the absence in the BRI of uniform standards to ensure the fair pricing of debt and agreed procedures to follow if a project fails. Relationships between China and host governments are also seen as important; joint involvement in project development and decision making, though desirable, is often lacking. Greater willingness on China's part to assist debtor countries to repay loans is also desirable – for example, it could help them develop product markets in China. As well, project managers should be more willing to use local sourcing to counter criticism that they rely too heavily on imported Chinese materials, equipment, and labour.

A potentially significant development in late 2018 that could ameliorate these risks was the agreement between President Xi and Japanese prime minister Shinzō Abe to embark on joint infrastructure projects as the two governments move to normalize their difficult political relationship. By engaging China in this way, Japan has recognized the opportunity to shape BRI strategy, gain added business for Japanese firms, and initiate a cooperative process with potentially positive geopolitical implications. Of even greater consequence, China's engaging with Japan could also help to address criticism that the BRI is a hidden long game in which China pursues its own agenda and geostrategic goals using Chinese-financed, Chinese-constructed transportation infrastructure to expand its military reach. Notably, unlike Italy's endorsement of the BRI, through which it seeks Chinese capital, Japan's overture initiates a new era of cooperation in building infrastructure.

What is less clear, while the BRI is enhancing these regions' economic potential through its emphasis on infrastructure, is whether the new investments will conform to Chinese standards and use Chinese technologies, including high-speed trains and data networks. Although still a distant prospect, some analysts have suggested that one day the BRI might challenge the Western rules-based order.[38]

Be that as it may, conduct of the April 2019 Belt and Road Forum illustrated some Chinese flexibility and a shift of emphasis to the BRI as a win-win proposition. One hundred countries attended the Forum, thirty-six of them sending their head of state. The Chinese host's tone was subdued even as officials reported Chinese companies had invested $90 billion in BRI projects and that, during the 2013–18 period, Chinese banks had extended $200–$300 billion in loans.[39] Xi Jingping's address was conciliatory, emphasizing the reform and opening measures announced at the 2019 session of the National People's Congress. These measures included expanding market access for foreign investors without Chinese partners, intensifying protection of intellectual property, ending forced technology transfers, engaging more in macroeconomic coordination and relying on market forces in renminbi valuation, and adopting a binding mechanism to honour agreed international laws and regulations.[40]

More immediately, attention is required to address the practical difficulties – including project selection, design, and risk management – of fully realizing the potential economic returns from BRI projects. Although debt distress is a risk, it can and should be managed according to internationally recognized standards, rather than leaving partner country institutions indebted to Chinese banks. As noted, there are early signs that Beijing is holding itself more accountable on these issues; with the BRI as the Chinese leader's signature global initiative, Beijing could hardly do anything less.

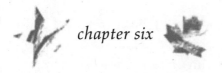

chapter six

LIVING WITH CHINA:
CANADA FINDS ITS WAY

Canada's relationship with China was transformed in 2018–19 following a period of drift and China's rejection in late 2017 of Canada's progressive trade agenda for bilateral free trade negotiations. China-US tensions had been rising as a bipartisan consensus formed that China was no longer a partner to engage with, but an assertive adversary that does not play fair. Huawei Technologies became the public face of techno-nationalist complaints about the role of the state in Chinese business. Canada entered the spotlight as the United States requested the arrest of Meng Wanzhou, Huawei's chief financial officer, under the terms of their bilateral extradition treaty. Canada's legal obligations counted for little, however, in the eyes of China's leaders, who were reportedly angered by this mistreatment of one of their elite. The Canada-China relationship plunged into a diplomatic deep freeze when Chinese authorities arrested two Canadians working in China, imposed a death sentence on a third charged with drug trafficking, blocked imports of canola, a grain that in 2017 accounted for 17 per cent of Canada's exports, and restricted other agricultural imports as well.

These developments underlined for Canadians several realities of life with China. First, they are not like us. China has great power aspirations and historical grievances. It punishes countries, particularly smaller ones, whose governments displease it, as with the arrests in 2014 of Canadians Kevin and Julia Garratt, and with Norway for awarding the Nobel Peace Prize to Liu Xiaobo in 2010. Second, Canada's bilateral options with China are influenced by the state of the China-US relationship, as became apparent in the 2018 US-Mexico-Canada Agreement (USMCA, the renamed NAFTA), to which the United States added an article imposing conditions on free trade negotiations with planned economies, such as China's, by any of the three signatories.[1] Third, restoring the relationship with China is a priority. In short, Canada needs a China strategy. Taking a comprehensive approach to the relationship argues against the current exclusive focus on the "comprehensive" free trade agreement that the United States has taken off the table and that likely would have taken many years to negotiate even if it had been possible. In this chapter, I begin by defining the China-US strategic context. I then propose a pragmatic, multipronged strategy that includes trade, investment, security, and engagement – a strategy based on mutual respect, accommodation, and willingness to discuss and manage deep differences in Canadian and Chinese values and institutions.

THE STRATEGIC CONTEXT

Their relationship with the United States dominates the strategic context in both Canada and China, but in different ways. Where Canada and the United States have many similar institutions and policies and their economies are deeply integrated, China and the United States are deeply different. Each views itself as exceptional. Even their sense of time differs, as might be expected when one country is a relative newcomer and the other a civilization dating back thousands of years. Chinese think in centuries, Americans in the short term. Their governance and conduct of relationships differ: Confucian philosophy prioritizes order and harmony; institutions of governance emphasize hierarchies and obligations. Americans' views, in contrast, are more transactional. Americans see their democratic capitalist system based on the rule of law, individual freedom, open markets and the separation of church and state as the best model for all countries. Views of government and the role of the state also differ. Americans tend to tolerate government as a necessity, but less is better; Chinese regard the state as essential to maintain harmony and order and to provide good governance.[2]

Both China and the United States have significant domestic economic and political challenges that are central policy priorities. Each is tackling these challenges, but in problematic ways that add to global uncertainty. In China the major economic reform agenda put forward at the Third Plenum in 2013 aimed to give the market a central role and produce a more sustainable, greener, services-oriented economy. The blueprint adopted at that time was subsequently superseded by other political priorities until 2018, when Xi Jinping's address to the Boao Forum signalled a return to economic reform and a commitment to innovation-driven growth and further market opening.[3] In contrast, since the 2016 election, the US administration's domestic priorities have focused on improving employment in manufacturing and a simplistic preoccupation with reducing bilateral trade deficits. Informal accounts by Western visitors meeting with senior Chinese officials in the first half of 2018 reported considerable confusion about US strategic objectives as possibly symptomatic of the decline of the United States and of the Western order. Others voiced concerns about US zero-sum thinking, observing that the United States' goal is to dominate – to isolate and contain China, promote internal divisions, and sabotage China's leadership.

Looking back, as the United States moved in 1972 to normalize relations and in 1979 to establish diplomatic relations, the rationale was that, despite their different systems, engaging China as it reformed and opened up would generate greater benefits than costs. That calculus has now changed with the proliferating evidence of

China's ambition to pursue innovation-driven growth using technologies that might contain someone else's intellectual property. China-US economic ties are fraying as the long-standing benefits of trade and investment are undermined by the costs to national security of such practices as China's forced technology transfers and the targeting of US technology firms by SOEs for investment and the theft of intellectual property. In response the United States is now attempting to isolate China through such measures as the aforementioned USMCA article, increased CFIUS scrutiny of Chinese investors, and increased export restrictions on strategically important technologies.[4] In short, Americans now believe Chinese are stealing their future, while Chinese believe Americans aim to contain China.

This zero-sum view dominated both the December 2017 release of the Trump administration's National Security Strategy and National Defense Strategy and Vice President Mike Pence's hard-hitting speech in October 2018.[5] These statements define China as a revisionist power seeking to challenge US influence, values, and interests.[6] Mistrust of China as a strategic rival is expressed across the political spectrum. In February 2019 a report by the Asia Society's Task Force on US-China Policy concluded that the two giants are on a collision course as the foundation of goodwill built up over many years erodes. As noted in Chapter 1, some dismiss such characterizations as stereotypical, maintaining that the real challenge comes from China's peacefully confronting the United States on its own terms – from its bid for greater influence and economic advantage in East Asia, a region that the United States has taken for granted. The real challenge also comes from China's promoting its own economic model while accepting global diversity, from pursuing its international interests within the existing order, but with governance reforms to increase its clout in the conduct of foreign policy.[7]

Standing back from the increasingly tense relationship, it is important to recall that zero-sum thinking is only one of several possible alternatives. As Graham Allison argues,[8] accommodation is one possibility, based on a serious search for an adjusted relationship and a new balance of power without military confrontation. Another option is to negotiate a long peace, along the lines of the Cold War détente, recognizing the importance of domestic priorities to both countries' leaders. A third option is to redefine the existing relationship of competition and cooperation to emphasize common global interests. For example, the United States could counter China's version of a new great power relationship with its own version, such as one that promotes cooperation on four great common threats: nuclear war, nuclear anarchy, terrorism, and climate change. Only one of these options is hostile, based on a strong US critique of the contradictions in communist ideology and its interest in undermining the regime and fomenting domestic instability.

Gideon Rachman, chief foreign affairs commentator for the *Financial Times*, has emphasized the institutional advantages for Western nations that underpin the existing global order. He argues that the world is still "wired through the West" in its control of interbank financial telecommunications and stable and secure Internet operations,[9] through the "wiring" provided by similar legal systems and common laws, and by the dollar as the world's main reserve currency. Unfortunately Western power has also been used to China's disadvantage. The long delay in reforming IMF governance to reflect China's increasing economic size and influence is a prominent example. China has pushed back, creating such alternative international financial institutions as the BRICs bank and the AIIB.

Sinologist Susan Shirk has argued that the two governments must work out a new modus operandi based on current realities. By 2030 China will have the world's largest economy; its total trade already outstrips that of the United States; and China is the de facto hub of the increasingly integrated economies of Asia, the world's fastest-growing region. China must also face the fact of the Party's fragile grip on power in the context of slowing growth and the risk of a financial crisis triggered by indebted SOEs and local governments. Shirk challenges China's triumphalism at escaping the global financial crisis, amid evidence of stalling SOE reforms, rising discrimination against foreign firms, and the clampdown on non-governmental activities and academic exchanges. Instead of co-operative leadership, we have seen China impose its sovereignty on its neighbours through its maritime claims.

Shirk focuses on living with China as it is. She counsels the United States to maintain and honour its alliances, be prepared to push back against discriminatory Chinese actions and laws, and recognize that China is not a unitary state. She emphasizes the importance of regular intergovernmental communication, and counsels Americans not to stoke antagonisms but to stand firm on China's advances in the South China Sea and insist on observance of international law. China, on the other hand, should address more effectively its ongoing discrimination against US investment by completing the long-delayed Bilateral Investment Treaty.

These expert insights and prescriptions are relevant to Canada's deeper engagement with China. As a middle power, Canada's choices for engagement are pragmatic ones with their own complexities. Given the depth of North American economic integration, evolving US perspectives of the China challenge will shape Canadian interests to some extent. Accommodation and cooperation with China is the preferred option. Under any scenario, Canada should emphasize the potential complementarities in the two countries' bilateral trade and investment. David Mulroney, former Canadian ambassador to China, argues that Canadians can respect China yet reject its discriminatory policies and contest its differing institutions and values.[10]

As a February 2019 poll of Canadians by the University of British Columbia School of Public Policy and Global Affairs revealed, however, many Canadians are confident the relationship can be managed even as negativity towards China grows. The poll revealed an even larger decline in favourable views of the United States.

Respondents identified expanding trade and investment as the top Canadian policy priority in the China relationship, with 64 per cent supporting a free trade agreement despite the decline in China's public image. Sixty-five per cent of respondents thought the current disputes would be managed and relations would revert to normal.[11]

CANADA'S NEED FOR A CHINA STRATEGY AND A NARRATIVE

Relations, however, might not return to normal. Canada needs a China strategy, one that incorporates these elements and is realistic and forward looking. Reducing dependence on the US market by diversifying trade and investment currently ranks high among Canada's national objectives. Yet it should be part of a more comprehensive strategy, one based on Canada's interests and long-term economic and security objectives. These strategic elements include careful definition of Canada's interests to be pursued in the China relationship, more emphasis in Canada on public learning about China, safeguarding Canada's national security and participating more actively in Asia's security order, widening and deepening bilateral economic engagement through trade and investment, and managing the long-term relationship with a more assertive China.[12]

Pursue Canada's Interests and Long-Term Goals

Leadership at the highest official levels is essential to build the long-term relationships with Chinese and other Asian leaders, as is customary in the region, that will serve Canada's interests. The two governments have pursued strategic links actively since 1970, when Canada recognized China's Communist government. In 2005 leaders agreed on a strategic partnership. Other official agreements facilitate tourism, financial services, transportation, and science and technology, while Memoranda of Understanding exist on the environment and nuclear cooperation. In 2014 the two governments signed a Foreign Investment Promotion and Protection Agreement (FIPA).

In 2016 the two leaders launched an Annual Dialogue between the Prime Minister of Canada and the Premier of China that began with each country's leader visiting the other. When Premier Li Keqiang visited Ottawa on 23 September 2016, a number of agreements were signed encouraging new areas of cooperation and establishing working groups and a renminbi trading hub in Canada. They also agreed to launch an Economic and Financial Strategic Dialogue at the vice-premier level. Attempts to initiate negotiations on a free trade agreement, however, failed to bear fruit in 2017. Complementing these economic initiatives were others in science, health, and public safety. Later in September, Beijing convened the inaugural meeting of the Canada-China High-Level Dialogue on National Security and the Rule of Law, where discussions began on improving bilateral cooperation.

Promote Public Learning about China

One goal for Canadian leaders' increased attention should be to deepen public knowledge about China and to address the reservations and concerns about China that have been voiced in recent opinion polls and in presentations to the Trudeau government's extensive 2017 public consultations on negotiating a free trade agreement.[13] Overall there is growing public support for a deeper economic relationship, but alarm about Chinese military activities and China's growing presence in Canada. Polling revealed public anxiety about cyber espionage and other issues seen as potential threats to jobs and the Canadian way of life. In the government's 2017 trade consultations, presenters called for engagement on human rights, cyber security, and regional security issues as expressions of Canadian values. They supported the emphasis on gender, environment, and labour standards in the progressive trade agenda – both as values and as differentiators between Canadians and their competitors in China.

The consultations attracted significant support from businesses and consumers in recognition of the substantial opportunities in the Chinese market and the realization that competitors in Australia and New Zealand are gaining strategic advantages, having already completed bilateral free trade agreements with China. Business presenters also called for greater predictability in China's trade restrictions in order to reduce the transactions costs they face in the Chinese market. Commercial and other stakeholders expressed concerns about the rule of law, and questioned China's willingness to adhere to its obligations negotiated in a comprehensive free trade agreement. Intellectual property protection was seen as improving, but the enforcement of rules as still problematic, suggesting the desirability of both a formal dispute settlement mechanism and mechanisms for dialogue. Concerns were also voiced about the complexities of doing business in a state-run economy populated by powerful SOEs.

These polls and consultations underline the need to address the outdated policy assumption that, as China develops and integrates into the world economy, it will become "more like us." China will be itself. Canadians should adjust their expectations by learning about it and living with it as it evolves. China's growing international presence and assertiveness with its Asian neighbours raises both hope and alarm. China insists it is pursuing what it defines as its core interests, but geopolitics clearly will be the central factor in the region's future.

Find a Narrative

An important contribution to the process of learning about China will be a narrative for deeper engagement that attracts public support. The narrative should reflect at least three realities. First, there are fundamental differences in the two countries' values and institutions. Deeper interaction will entail risks and frictions that must be recognized and managed. Editorials urge Canada's leaders, as they deepen economic and security ties, to be realistic about whom they are dealing with and not to ignore fundamental differences, as Chinese officials do. Second, Canadians need to be clear about the potential implications for their country's relationship with the United States as Canada diversifies its trade and deepens integration with what the United States now officially sees as a strategic rival. Third, although China might be a major US competitor and might wish to rewrite the rules, it has become a player in the larger objective of a peaceful and cooperative world order, to which Xi Jinping has emphasized his commitment.

A narrative for deeper engagement with China should therefore accept that *China is different, but cooperation is possible and differences can be acknowledged and managed. Canada's permanent reality is its location and deep integration with the US economy, but diversifying trade and foreign relationships serves Canada's long-term interests. The Chinese market is a logical focus but should not become a new source of dependence.*

Canadians could learn from Australia's bilateral relationship with China, developed over four decades, aided by public leadership, education, learning about how to deal with a different governing system, advocacy, and exchanges of people. A key differentiating factor, of course, is that China is Australia's largest neighbour and economic partner, not the United States, with which Canada's economy is so deeply integrated.

Canada could also increase the opportunities for learning about China by expanding exchanges among members of civil society and by funding study programs for students, along the lines of the US-based "100 Thousand Strong" initiative to raise the number of students studying abroad. In Canada, *Global Education for Canadians*, published in November 2017 by the University of Ottawa and University of Toronto, provides a blueprint for similarly equipping

Canadians to function in a globalized world.[14] Such exchanges should be backed by the deeper connections between leaders suggested above.

Finally, care should be taken to recognize and integrate other key dimensions of the bilateral relationship, particularly in security, in recognition of the new realities of China-US geostrategic tensions and of China's growing influence in the rest of the world.

Safeguard National Security and Participate in Asia's Security Order

Security has two main dimensions: the safeguarding of Canada's own national security, and Canada's potential contribution to the nascent security order in the Asian region.

The implications for national security policy of a deeper Canada-China economic relationship are becoming more apparent as Chinese firms pursue mergers and acquisitions transactions in Canada. Cyber security and telecommunications infrastructure are two particular concerns. Canada and China have signed a cyber security agreement that prohibits state-to-state attacks, but two recent transactions in the telecommunications sector raise questions about the security implications of the acquisition of Canadian assets by Chinese enterprises. One transaction was the successful bid in 2017 for Norsat, a satellite communications supplier, by Chinese communications giant Hytera. This transaction was completed despite opposition from US lawmakers who argued against allowing a Canadian supplier to the US Defense Department to be acquired by a Chinese firm that is partly owned by the Chinese government and is an instrument of the Chinese state. The second transaction was the bid by SOE China Communications Construction Co. to acquire Aecon, a large, publicly listed Canadian construction firm, a transaction that the Canadian government blocked in 2018 on national security grounds. Since certain Aecon assets are part of the telecommunications infrastructure in both Canada and the United States, it was feared that transferring them to a Chinese-owned enterprise risked leakage of defence technology to the Chinese state.

Both Huawei Technologies, a privately owned company, and ZTE, its state-owned competitor, have been banned by Australia, New Zealand, and the United States from supplying equipment to 5G wireless networks. Canada is being pressed to do the same.[15] Public safety minister Ralph Goodale initiated a government-wide evaluation of the security of supply chains, as have other members of the so-called Five Eyes intelligence-sharing alliance consisting of Australia, Canada, New Zealand, the United Kingdom, and the United States. Both Canada and the United Kingdom have agencies tasked with conducting security tests. In Canada the Communications Security Establishment has tested Huawei's telecommunications equipment for such supply chain cyber threats as software vulnerabilities that can be exploited or pre-installed as malware in equipment or software. The UK government has permitted Huawei to undertake a limited range of activities, excluding it from supplying the 5G network "core" and government activities and subjecting it to continuous system monitoring.

As noted, Huawei in Canada has been caught up in the intensifying adversarial China-US relationship. The United States aims to exclude Chinese firms from US business, and is pressing Canada to do likewise. Canadian telecom firms BCE and Telus, however, depend heavily on Huawei equipment in their networks, and argue that a ban on such procurement would reduce their options – leaving only Nokia and Ericsson to choose from – and raise their costs. Their argument is that US demands are based primarily on US security arguments that ignore the economic issues, and they question the US case for the ban as protectionist and politically motivated. They argue that security concerns about Huawei's 5G switching systems can be dealt with by requiring its compliance with national regulations, as Germany has reportedly done, and by limiting Huawei connections to core voice and data networks.[16] Others disagree, sometimes vehemently, arguing, for example, that using Huawei equipment would be "giving the Chinese Communist Party the power to spy on our daily lives on Canadian soil."[17]

Huawei also figures in growing concerns about cyber security and protection of intellectual property in a digital world. Huawei's support for Canadian research in 5G wireless technology has attracted public scrutiny on the grounds that Canadian researchers who transfer intellectual property to Huawei as a quid pro quo for research funding are creating national security concerns. Critics assert that research institutions that receive such funding are likely to become dependent on a technology firm that could be required to transfer technologies used in national and Five Eyes networks to the Chinese state, thereby undermining the security of Western networks. Canadian universities claim they are actively managing intellectual property issues, noting that Canada's lack of large, innovative firms of Huawei's size leaves Canadian researchers few choices for participating in developing cutting-edge technology if they wish to remain in Canada, while not facilitating such research could harm Canada's own long-term interests. Concerns should also be allayed by the Canadian Centre for Cyber Security's conclusion that Canada has a robust system to test for and prevent security breaches.[18]

These cases illustrate the importance of Canada's ability to manage the relationships among security, international trade, and investment. They also raise questions about US strategy with respect to Huawei. If the goal is to destroy the company, rather than reform it, the US push to exclude China could have the opposite effect: China could double down on technological innovation and its entry into markets where the United States is relatively absent, creating through time two competing and technologically differentiated "blocs." This is particularly possible in telecommunications, where Huawei is a world leader. Experienced voices, including those of Singapore's Kishore Mahbubani and Geoff Mulgan of NESTA, the

UK Innovation Foundation, are among those who argue that, since the rest of the world will adapt and make room for China, a more effective strategy would be to push for a multilateral governance framework that China would be interested in joining. Such an institution should address the need for internationally accepted boundaries for cyber warfare and multilateral rules of conduct.[19]

The second security dimension is regional security in Asia.[20] Here Canada has a window of opportunity to play a constructive role as Asians search for the leadership and institutions needed to address the risks and tensions of China's rising profile. Until recently, China regarded international institutions and norms created by Western countries in the post-war period as generally in accordance with its interests. China has been a responsible player in international efforts to address climate change and in responding to natural disasters and pandemics. It has complied with the treaties it has signed, and has been active in all of the Asia-Pacific regional institutions. It has signed a number of free trade agreements with its neighbours, and has initiated an APEC-led process that could lead to a Free Trade Area of the Asia and the Pacific.

China is not out to overturn the existing order. As President Xi has emphasized in his speeches at Davos and elsewhere since he chaired the 2016 Hangzhou G20 summit, we live in an increasingly interdependent world. But as he also made clear at the 19th Party Congress in 2017, China will be more assertive in influencing the rules of international institutions. In the past, China has been a participant in these institutions, but not a leader. Xi has extolled the virtues of Chinese socialist democracy, and has reacted to the inertia in global institutions by projecting China's influence through its own institutions, such as the Shanghai Cooperation Organization, the New Development Bank, and the Asian Infrastructure Investment Bank.

At the same time, the regional conversation is shifting from the design of individual institutions to questions about the structure of the regional security order and the leadership required. These questions are of particular interest to the region's middle powers, including Australia, New Zealand, South Korea, Indonesia, and Malaysia. Anticipating increased China-US tensions, they are asking what adjustments are needed by the great powers to maximize accommodation, show restraint, and offer reassurance to others in the region. What are the right venues for working out the norms, rules, and practices of a new security order? Non-traditional security through cooperation on humanitarian assistance, disaster relief, and search and rescue are priorities as well. Canadian civil society has the reputation, credibility, and domestic resources to be a leader in working with China and other countries on such matters as water management, climate change adaptation and mitigation, infectious disease prevention, and the management of geopolitical tensions, including in the Arctic.

Yet Canada's recent record has been one of strategic silence – a spectator in these regional discussions even though the consequences of a direct military clash between the region's great powers or a new China-US cold war would be devastating for global supply chains and for Canada's commercial interests. Unless Canada is a multidimensional player, it will not be accepted as a participant in regional initiatives to dampen geopolitical rivalry or to set the region's cooperative framework and rules. Even if Canada chooses a reactive approach, that should be articulated so that partners know what to expect.

Canadians believe their interests are best served by a rules-based order and open regional institutions, rather than by competing regional structures. Competing regionalisms could lead to exclusive blocs led by either the United States or China, and make sense to those who still think in narrow terms of strategic rivalry and balance of power. But such competition would miss a historic opportunity to generate collective benefits of deepening regional economic integration. Canada, working with others, should be prepared to prevent miscalculations and accidents or rivalry that could spill over into conflict. As a middle power, Canada's past role was to bridge great power differences whenever possible, not to exacerbate them. Accommodation to find common ground requires judicious decisions in the search for ways to adjust rules and institutions to reflect the views and interests of Asia's rising powers, and China.

Widen and Deepen Economic Engagement

In contrast to its relative silence on security issues, Canada has been active in economic and commercial relationships with China and its Asian neighbours. China now accounts for 18 per cent of global nominal GDP and 40 per cent of Asia's GDP (in terms of purchasing power parity). China is also now Canada's second-largest national trading partner,[21] accounting for 7 per cent of its total trade (Figure 6.1), 4 per cent of its exports, and nearly 12 per cent of imports – in contrast, the US market accounts for 65 per cent of Canada's total trade and 75 per cent of its exports. Unlike Canada's trade with the United States, however, with its intense competition and deep integration through supply chains, Canada's trade with China is largely complementary and provides the basis for long-term collaboration.

The potential benefits of building on these complementarities were recognized in the *Canada-China Economic Complementarities Study*,[22] published in 2012. China relies on imports of food, energy, and natural resources; Canada's comparative advantage lies in its rich natural endowments. China's strategic industries include clean energy sources, conservation, and renewables, where Canadians are becoming innovators. The two governments have a chance to build upon these complementarities if they negotiate a trade-liberalizing agreement. Restrictions on free trade with China imposed by the USMCA do not have to be an inhibiting factor because in this case

Figure 6.1 Canada's Total Trade with Selected Asian Economies, 2000–16

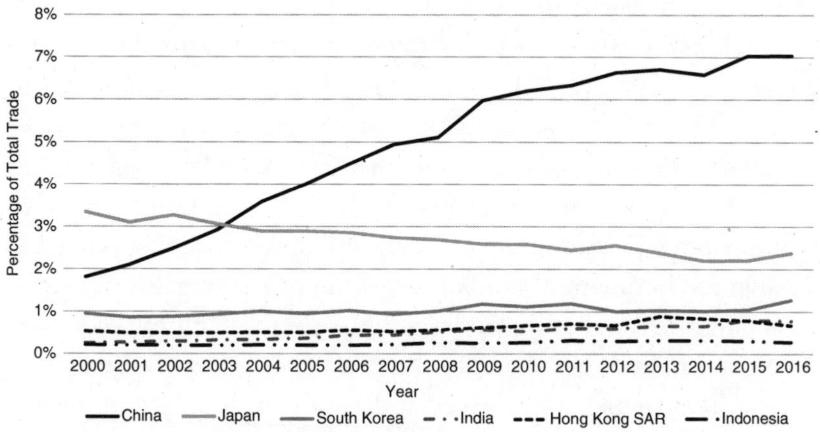

Sources: Merchandise trade data: adapted from Canada, "Trade Data Online," available online at https://www.ic.gc.ca/app/scr/tdst/tdo/crtr.html?productType= NAICS&lang=eng, accessed 14 September 2018; service trade data: adapted from Statistics Canada, "International Transactions in Services, by Selected Countries, annual (x 1,000,000)," table 36-10-0007-01, available online at http://www5.statcan.gc.ca/ cansim/a26?lang=eng&retrLang=eng&id=3760036&paSer=&pattern=&stByVal=1&p1= 1&p2=-1&tabMode=dataTable&csid=, accessed 14 September 2018.

there are alternative – and more appropriate – approaches and agreements than comprehensive free trade.

Making the Chinese market a Canadian priority is desirable for at least three reasons. One is the uncertain future of the bilateral relationship with the United States under President Trump's zero-sum, protectionist approach. Second, new competitors are lined up to supply China with food, energy, and natural resources; China's free trade agreement with Australia, for example, grants concessional market access for Australian meat, wine, and seafood, which provides Australian competitors price advantages over Canadian suppliers. Third, the MIC 2025 strategy encourages import substitution to help Chinese enterprises move up global value chains in manufacturing and services. The implication is that Chinese producers in such industries as advanced rail transport equipment expect to do what Canadians already do well.

The list of sectors in which complementarities provide opportunities for collaboration is a long one.[23] The energy sector could be a game changer for the bilateral relationship. China is the world's largest net importer of petroleum and other liquid fuels, and seeks to tap Canada's generous endowments of these products. In addition, with the priority accorded non-fossil fuels as China pursues a cleaner environment, Canadian firms can offer expertise and products ranging from hydroelectric and nuclear to uranium production to oil and natural gas. Canada also has expertise in energy conservation, renewables, clean tech, and managing the environmental effects of energy production. The challenge is to link this expertise to Asian supply chains.

Food security in China provides another complementary opportunity given Canada's abundant food-supply capabilities. China is in transit from traditional to modern agriculture, while Canada has made large investments in innovation, technology, and practices to increase agricultural productivity. Pork is already a fast-growing export, as is cooperation on pig genetics.

The Belt and Road Initiative offers further opportunities for cooperation in infrastructure and transportation. Canadian firms have globally recognized expertise in land- and marine-based transportation technologies, in construction and construction machinery, and in building materials. China's large air services industry and Canada's record of exporting aerospace products and technical and management skills are another complementarity.

Beyond these sectors are other services industries, including tourism and education. The China Outbound Tourism Research Institute reports that by 2017 Chinese tourists were making 145 million cross-border trips annually. Canada is already an education destination as parents prepare their children for the highly competitive national tests in China and for possible futures in international businesses and organizations. Recent clampdowns on academic freedom can only add to the advantages of educating children abroad.

With the growth of China's middle class, we can also expect rising demand for health care, environmental services, transportation, and financial services, all of which Canadians do well. Canada has a strong reputation for successful management of the effects of the global financial crisis and for the diverse investments by its large pension funds around the globe, including in China. As noted, Canada was also a first mover in establishing the first renminbi hub in the Western hemisphere to facilitate financial transactions between the US dollar and the Chinese currency in low-risk trade and investment.

The other significant complementarity is in cross-border investments in productive assets. Major Canadian investors in large, well-established companies in China include Manulife, Sun Life, Bank of Montreal, Bombardier, and SNC-Lavalin, which have created Chinese affiliates over the years. More recently pension funds have acquired Chinese and other Asian assets in public and private equities and real estate. Even so, the stock of Canadian investment in China pales in comparison with investments in the United States – and in comparison with Chinese inflows to Canada. The latter have grown rapidly since 2008 (Figure 6.2) and have stimulated a policy debate that is discussed below.

As a scene setter, a question can be asked about the potential fate of Canadian trade and investment in sectors where Canadians have developed new technologies, such as clean tech, energy conservation, transportation services, and agri-foods. What should be Canada's strategy with respect to MIC 2025's alleged emphasis on acquiring foreign technologies and forcing technology transfers? These threats might diminish in response to intense US pressure at the China-US trade talks in early 2019 to abandon such practices.

Figure 6.2 FDI Stocks in Canada, by Investing Country, 2000–17

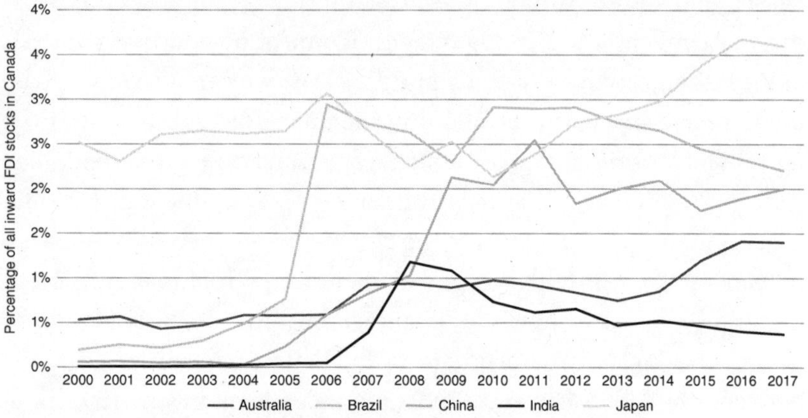

Source: Statistics Canada, "International Investment Position, Canadian Direct Investment Abroad and Foreign Direct Investment in Canada, by Country, Annual (× 1,000,000," table 36-10-0008-01, available online at http://www5.statcan.gc.ca/cansim/a26?lang=eng&retrLang=eng&id=3760051&paSer=&pattern=&stByVal=1&p1=1&p2=-1&tabMode=dataTable&csid=, accessed 10 May 2019.

Negotiate Bilateral Investment and Trade Regimes with China

Investment: Although FDI inflows from China in recent years have included large numbers of small investments by privately owned Chinese enterprises – up to 2007 almost all investments were from large SOEs – industry players remain concerned about the steep learning curve Chinese investors face, even when their commercial objectives are similar to those of other investors. Differences in regulatory regimes and rules of the road are not fully appreciated or addressed.

In 2014 Canada and China agreed to a Foreign Investment Promotion and Protection Agreement (FIPA). Initially hailed as a big step forward in ensuring investors in each country are treated as well as domestic investors, the FIPA also provides a comprehensive dispute resolution mechanism and protects foreign investors' ability to repatriate capital and income. But weaknesses in the agreement have generated criticism. On the Canadian side, the Investment Canada Act imposes restrictions on Chinese investments above specified monetary thresholds. On the Chinese side, potential Canadian investors are not protected from discrimination in the pre-establishment phase of business development. China's proposed new law on foreign investment would address such issues by introducing new standards, greater transparency, and a more open and predictable environment for investors.

Over the 2008–14 period, the small stock of Chinese FDI in Canada grew rapidly, and was the subject of an ongoing policy debate on three issues. Of these, ownership was the most contentious because of the predominance of Chinese SOEs and the concern that SOE investment decisions are based on political, rather than commercial, criteria. A second issue was reciprocal market access for Canadians in China, who do not have access comparable to that enjoyed by Chinese investors in Canada. A third issue was national security. SOEs are a source of particular concern. Since 2008 most prominent Chinese investments and acquisitions in Canada have been carried out by SOEs in the energy and mining sectors. Privately owned enterprises have invested mainly in minerals and coal, chemicals, solar power, and telecommunications equipment. But as we saw in Chapter 4, much merger and acquisitions activity is once again dominated by SOEs as China's regulators move to reduce systemic risks in the financial system and strengthen SOEs by forcing their consolidation.

FDI has a number of benefits, not least because investments are long-term decisions requiring deeper engagement than cross-border trade. But there are also the risks of transferring control of strategic assets and technologies and of cyber espionage. Canada, the United States, and Australia screen inbound FDI and mergers and acquisitions to ensure such transactions do not pose a national security threat. The European Union is more open, although this is now changing in response to rising Chinese inflows and growing Chinese interest in acquiring advanced technologies.

Canada's investment screening regime is risk oriented and ranked by the OECD as restrictive and more opaque relative to those of other OECD countries (but less so than China's). A decision by Prime Minister Stephen Harper in December 2012 to restrict SOEs from owning controlling stakes in Canadian oil sands companies – except in (undefined) "exceptional circumstances" – added a third test to an already-opaque net benefits test and national security screen. Although the intent was to address the risk of (SOE) investors' applying political, rather than market-based, criteria in their decisions, the policy change had a chilling effect on investment that disadvantaged the energy industry in a period of unusually low oil prices. Rather than influence SOEs' behaviour, it risked sending a message to privately owned enterprises that they are not welcome in Canada.

Rationalizing Canada's three investment screens into a single, more transparent national security test likely would tighten export controls over some technologies while reducing the transaction costs of the current uncertain approval process. Existing restrictions also discourage private equity players, who look to large companies for exit strategies from risky but innovative investments in small companies, and who in turn lack access to large players' global supply chains.[24]

In summary, Canada's investment screening regime should focus mainly on national security issues. It should be transparent and target investors' behaviour, rather than ownership.

Trade: The public consultations in 2017 described earlier focused on negotiations on a bilateral free trade agreement. In 2015 Chinese officials had suggested a quick negotiation that might closely follow the China-Australia agreement signed in June that year. But standards for agreements have shifted since then, with Canada's signing both the Comprehensive Trade and Economic Agreement (CETA) with the European Union in 2016 and the renamed Comprehensive and Progressive Agreement for Trans-Pacific Partnership (TPP) in

2017. Both agreements include services and investment, with more sophisticated coverage than the China-Australia deal – which itself is considered to be a "living" agreement requiring periodic upgrading.

When they met in September 2016, Canadian and Chinese leaders committed to regular high-level contact as the foundation for deeper economic and security relationships. They identified twenty-nine areas of agreement and cooperation, the fourth of which was "to launch exploratory discussions for a possible Canada-China Free Trade Agreement."[25] The 2014 FIPA is a useful precedent and a potential building block for any agreement. But a comprehensive free trade agreement is an ambitious goal: China has only a few such agreements with developed economies, and none was negotiated overnight. In decade-long negotiations with South Korea and Australia, major issues included differing regulatory, legal, and institutional factors and the scale of adjustment burdens that labour in less-competitive sectors likely would face. The South Korean negotiation was completed by temporarily setting aside investment in order to liberalize trade in goods and services in a timely fashion.

Canada's interests would be served by moving forward promptly in recognition of increased competition in the Chinese market as the China-Australia agreement is phased in. With tariff removals agreed to on 95 per cent of goods exports, Australians expected the deal to add the equivalent of C$20 billion to bilateral trade in four years, particularly in agriculture, natural resources, energy, manufacturing, and services.[26] Without comparable concessions, Canadians are at a disadvantage.

A bilateral negotiation will be neither easy nor straightforward because of the differences in economic systems and the range of trade and non-trade issues involved. Canada should be prepared for negotiations influenced by unique Chinese practices and concerns about Canadian policies. For example, Canadians are familiar with Chinese criticisms of their inability to find consensus among various interest groups around adding more pipeline capacity to transport Alberta's oil and natural gas to world markets beyond the United States. Criticism can also be expected of Canada's investment screening policies and the prohibition in 2012 of future acquisitions by SOEs of Canadian firms in the oil sands sector. Although the policy applies to all SOEs regardless of nationality, criticism of the opacity of Canada's overall regime continues.

Trade Negotiating Options: In theory Canada has several options for structuring negotiations, but not all would accommodate the progressive trade agenda and its non-trade issues. This is likely true of the option suggested by Chinese officials who favour a largely goods-only agreement similar to the agreement with Australia. The second option, to seek a "high-standard" version of Canada's negotiations in the CETA and TPP talks, would be a better fit. This route would be challenging for both parties to negotiate, however, as it would require detailed knowledge of each country's institutions and policies. Either of these alternatives would also be an outright free trade agreement, and therefore subject to the conditions on free trade negotiations with planned economies imposed by the USMCA. A third option would be to embark on a phased, longer-term sectoral approach. This option would be time consuming, but it would give both sides needed opportunities to learn about the other, and it would avoid USMCA strictures.

The first option provides the clearest and simplest way to proceed, and, in the absence of the USMCA, likely would avoid most difficult regulatory and institutional issues. As in the 2015 China-Australia agreement, tariffs could be reduced in agriculture, natural resources, and manufacturing, trade in services could be facilitated, and barriers to Chinese private investment in Canada lowered.[27] Australia committed to phase in tariff reduction beginning with 85 per cent removal, increasing to 95 per cent of goods exports upon full implementation of the agreement. China committed to eliminating tariffs on 10–25 per cent of such products as meat, wine, and seafood, and to improving Australian firms' access to the Chinese market. But China also insisted on exclusions of products important to food security and the protection of wood and paper products. In addition China "paid" for continued protection of some other sensitive sectors by dropping demands for investment.[28]

The second approach would be similar to the first in that it would seek to eliminate Chinese tariffs and improve market access for Canada's goods and services by applying the principle of national treatment. Canada's goal presumably would be to achieve concessions similar to those agreed in the CETA and TPP negotiations.[29] This would involve negotiating a "high-standard" agreement along the lines of the TPP, and would require extensive cooperation among officials in "Canada-China FTA committees" in which officials would engage on regulatory cooperation and problem solving during the negotiations and afterwards during implementation. CETA and TPP chapters could also be used as models in such sectors as sanitary and phytosanitary measures (CETA, Chapter 5; TPP, Chapter 14 for e-commerce and digital trade, Chapter 18 for intellectual property protection, and Chapter 16 for competition policy). Canada should also be prepared to deal with Chinese demands for a more transparent and less discriminatory investment screening regime and access to government procurement, and to accord China market economy status.

The third option would be a step-by-step approach resembling the Economic Partnership Agreements that are often used among East Asian nations. Unlike a free trade agreement, which aims to remove substantially all trade barriers, an Economic Partnership Agreement is less demanding, but is a flexible vehicle that facilitates ongoing liberalization and deeper economic cooperation. Such an agreement also allows for exceptions – as Canada experienced in negotiations with Japan, where agricultural sensitivities on both sides were potential roadblocks to a comprehensive approach. China is also familiar with Economic Partnership Agreements as a participant in the Regional Comprehensive Economic Partnership, a major economic negotiation – mainly concerning goods – that is ongoing among the ten-member Association of Southeast Asian Nations (ASEAN) and six countries with which ASEAN has free trade agreements.

Canadian and Chinese officials laid some significant groundwork for this kind of approach in the 2012 *Complementarities Study*, which selected seven sectors for analysis of trade patterns and existing trade and investment barriers, as well as for complementarities and opportunities for growth.[30] In 2018 the Public Policy Forum further developed this approach with its proposal for a strategic framework for deepening bilateral integration in its report, *Diversification not Dependence: A Made-in-Canada China Strategy.*[31]

Such an approach, however, would take time to negotiate. In several sectors, both parties would face tariff and non-tariff barriers to various goods or services – for example, in the treatment of vegetable oils and seeds, in which Canada has an interest. In some sectors, the parties could cooperate around common interests, such as by removing *intra*-sectoral barriers; in other instances, removal of barriers would have to be addressed through *inter*-sectoral negotiations, where tradeoffs would be possible. This analytic approach would help to identify areas of common interest, where the mutual confidence necessary to conclude a more comprehensive arrangement could be developed with carefully sequenced cooperation in chosen sectors. Obviously the necessary mutual learning would be facilitated if the process began with a focus on sectors where bilateral cooperation is already under way. Clean tech and environmental goods and services would be an obvious candidate; agriculture and agri-food would be another, although tariffs would be an obstacle, as the following sectoral summaries illustrate.[32]

Sectoral Examples: Clean tech and environmental goods and services would be a leading candidate for an Economic Partnership

Agreement approach given the two countries' existing level of bilateral cooperation, the sector's high importance to China, and Canada's growing commitment to it. Beginning the formal process with a cooperative agreement in this sector could establish the mutual confidence and trust needed to deal with more difficult issues such as agriculture, where there are competing interests. In clean tech and environmental goods and services, both parties have demonstrated their interest in addressing domestic and global challenges. Trade in goods is small but growing fast. China imports clean tech goods from Canada – particularly parts and components for wind power generators and smart grids – while Canada imports solar cells. Cooperation takes the form of science and technology partnerships and initiatives to match Canadian capacity to Chinese needs.

Company size is a potential barrier to growth in this cooperation, in that Canadian companies are often small and medium-sized enterprises that operate on a small scale relative to the solutions Chinese customers seek. Intellectual property protection is an additional concern. Since 2016, however, clean tech has become a policy priority for both parties, with financial commitments to innovation, R&D, support for project finance, working capital, and equity investments, and assistance to commercialize clean technologies. In recognition of the relatively small size of many Canadian firms, a number of government departments have contributed to a Clean Growth Hub to provide one-stop services.

This high level of mutual interest implies the possibility of an agreement on environmental cooperation, perhaps as a side agreement similar to the North American Agreement on Environmental Cooperation in NAFTA in which both parties committed to enforce their own domestic laws. A council on environmental cooperation might also be created to foster partnerships between Canada's clean tech firms and Chinese firms in the effort, among others, to facilitate inputs into the global supply chains of original equipment manufacturers' international operations.

The agriculture and agri-food sector is also high on the list in the *Complementarities Study*, yet there are good reasons to discuss this sector later in the overall sequence of negotiations. Although there is ongoing cooperation in international forums, as well as bilateral mechanisms and agreements covering biotechnology, sustainable agriculture, and food safety, there are significant barriers to trade. Tariffs are still high in both countries (China's are 15.6 per cent, Canada's 11.3 per cent), and exceptions exist in certain product areas such as dairy, where Canada's protection of its market prevents exports of any significance. Concessions made in the CETA and TPP negotiations would loosen this restrictive regime somewhat. Regulatory obstacles exist, with both sides identifying sanitary and phytosanitary measures and differing standards that raise uncertainties and trade costs. Negotiating tariff reductions and addressing product exceptions from negotiations, as Canada did with softwood lumber in the NAFTA negotiations – "paying" for the agreement's dispute resolution compromise by opening energy to regional free trade – would be a high-stakes affair. Tradeoffs across sectors likely would be necessary, and therefore better dealt with as the negotiations mature.

Sequencing: These sectoral initiatives could be first steps in a sequenced or 'living' agreement that is renegotiated and modernized through time. Sequencing should be guided by a clear set of principles: that bargaining is consistent with the WTO and observes the principles of non-discrimination and national treatment. The goal should be to reduce and eventually eliminate barriers to trade in goods, services, and investment. Indeed a larger framework for the end game would be essential to allow the inevitable tradeoffs involved in inter-sectoral bargaining. For example, tariffs in one sector could be reduced by one of the parties in exchange for reductions by the other party in another sector.

In 2016 the two governments created a cooperative context when they agreed to double two-way visits and bilateral trade by 2025 and to improve the environment for cooperation in agriculture, energy, manufacturing, financial services, and infrastructure. Aviation, air transport, educational, and health care services were also included. To ensure the sequencing process is forward looking, talks might be structured to provide a platform for defining new rules if needed as new technologies emerge, such as those in biotechnology, robotics and digitalization, artificial intelligence, and machine learning. Further, if the agreement included a separate chapter on investment, as in the TPP, provisions for the settlement of investor-state disputes could be improved. Provisions should allow governments the right to regulate to achieve public policy objectives, while transparency standards should be required for documents filed with cases, and rosters of arbitrators should be subjected to strict standards to prevent conflicts of interest.

China would be a unique partner in such a negotiation. Rules for implementation would need to make explicit that neither party will impose ad hoc regulatory restrictions after negotiations are completed – as happened in the China-Australia agreement, where China reinterpreted some features when the deal took effect during a period of market price volatility. In the event that China failed to honour or reinterpreted its commitments, Canada should consider adopting special reciprocal measures to hold both parties accountable.

In summary, China will remain different even as its global economic and political prominence grows. Trade liberalization, which tends to dominate the debate about deeper economic integration, is now about much more than reducing tariffs and quotas on goods. With the proliferation of services trade and investment in global value chains, trade negotiations now include a number of formerly "behind the border" domestic policies, such as competition and investment policies, that call for ways to address regulatory differences and transparency and reduce administrative burdens of trade in China. More sensitive issues could also be addressed through cooperative discussions and the use of side letters to an Economic Partnership Agreement.

Addressing Non-trade Issues: Increasingly, political pressures are being brought to bear in trade negotiations to include non-trade issues and find ways to engage that bridge differences in values and institutions. The Canada-China negotiation is no exception, as the Trudeau government discovered in December 2017 when the Chinese leader showed no interest in its progressive trade agenda's proposals for gender equality, environmental protection, and labour standards. Such agenda items do not fit readily into negotiations structured to deal with the usual trade issues of tariffs, quotas, and other trade restrictions. Instead alternative cooperative approaches have been developed, such as CETA's policy dialogues, which provide channels to exchange information and find ways to cooperate on non-trade issues of common interest, such as peace and security, counterterrorism, human rights, migration, and sustainable development. Canadians have considered proposing a bilateral forum on human rights to highlight the importance of international obligations on human rights standards and to address specific concerns, such as China's treatment of its Uighur minority.[33] Other options include linking labour standards and environmental protection to the negotiations through separate Memoranda of Understanding or through dialogues intended to exchange views on current and potential policies and practices. Australia has long experience with alternative forums for such exchanges.

Manage the Relationship with an Increasingly Assertive China

China has punished Canada for acting under the terms of Canada's bilateral extradition treaty with the United States and arresting Huawei executive Meng Wanzhou. Meng's case will wind its way through the Canadian judicial system; in its wake, Canadians will need to push patiently and persistently for normalizing the relationship with China.

Reactions have been mixed. The 2018/2019 Canada-China Business Survey of businesses in the respective countries reported that 20 per cent of respondents had been negatively affected by the dispute. Respondents from both countries had changed their business plans and cancelled investments.[34] But not all Chinese are angry with Canada. Chinese consumers set new records during the 2019 spring festival in their demand for Canadian products – notably seafood, but also tourism. Chinese visa applications to Canada reportedly increased in 2018, with December being the second-busiest month in two years.[35] A Canadian company reportedly has won a procurement contract with the AIIB, and others are bidding for contracts as well.[36]

As noted earlier, the Asia Society's task Force on US-China Policy reports a changing US view of China towards one in which China observes the rules of world order when it is in its interest to do so. But, as the Task Force emphasizes, replacing engagement with an adversarial relationship is in no one's interest. Some assert that Xi Jinping's goal is global dominance; others argue that he is diversifying the available "portfolio" of international institutions and systems, thereby increasing his options.[37] Those who argue his goal is global dominance point to China's use of "sharp" power abroad through influence on the diaspora exerted by the United Front Work Department of the CCP.[38] Evidence that China is moving beyond the exercise of soft power appears in reports of the purchase of political influence and support for political candidates in certain countries.[39] Confucius Institutes, once welcomed, now face accusations of restraining or shaping countries' national debates about China. In Australia, New Zealand, and at the United Nations, there are rising concerns about Chinese political pressures on politicians and participants in policy debates. Australia has passed sweeping national security legislation banning foreign interference and making it a crime to damage Australian economic relations with another country.[40] In February 2019 the relationship reached a new level of pushback when the Australian government revoked a Chinese businessman's residency and denied him citizenship as penalties for political activities and buying influence in Australia.[41] Evidence of intimidation of Chinese students and of their reporting on one another has surfaced on US campuses as well. Creeping censorship threatens academic and journalistic freedom, with one university press facing blockage of online access in China to politically sensitive articles from a China-focused journal.[42]

This evidence of increasing assertiveness and opportunism underlines the significance of balancing engagement and accommodation with pushback by alliances among governments and coalitions among civil society and the media. The evidence suggests that China's commitment to accommodation is conditional on its compatibility with the Party's compact with the people. There are sceptics, however, such as former ambassador David Mulroney, who has called for "smart" engagement that reduces dependence on Chinese demand for Canada's agricultural products and adds more value in Canada. He argues for greater selectivity in civil exchanges and tourism and for adopting a firmer stance towards sources of Chinese influence. Such measures are likely to attract criticism from Beijing and require determined responses.[43]

Conclusion

In early 2019 the future of Canada's relationship with China is uncertain. In a complex policy environment, Canada needs a China strategy based on long-term economic and security objectives.

As the Chinese economy approaches parity in size with that of the United States, Xi Jinping has abandoned Deng Xiaoping's "hide and bide" strategy for an assertive posture and messages that appear to challenge US pre-eminence and to support more state intervention in the economy. Calm voices in China counselling that the smart response to US pressures is to "double down on opening up" have little effect, even though such a strategy could avoid a costly and self-defeating trade war, and support China's long-term growth objectives.

China's mix of state intervention and market forces has caused tensions evident throughout the analysis in this book. Tensions among policymakers arise because of the increasing official intervention in "made-in-China" innovation, despite evidence that such top-down direction is likely to inhibit the risk-taking necessary to develop innovative ideas – and despite evidence that Chinese state-owned enterprises are less productive than their privately owned competitors. Tensions with the US government increased in early May 2019 when what appeared to be a trade deal broke down. Officials on both sides, under intense political pressures to be tough, reached an impasse. Chinese officials sought a deal between equals, while Americans, who now regard China as a strategic rival, were using tariff threats to press for changes in China's economic system, something colonial powers had sought in the past. At the same time, China's leaders had short-term concerns to modernize the financial system and improve the business environment, particularly for small and medium-sized enterprises and for the private sector. Without such changes, China's short-term prospects are mixed. The return of the state, politicization of markets, and increased repression have sent mixed messages to key sectors, reduced China's long-term growth prospects, and might weaken the implicit social contract between the Party and the people.

Although China has penalized Canada harshly for participating in the US government's moves against Huawei, Canada, like other trading partners of both the United States and China, stands to benefit from the liberalizing effect of the new Chinese law on FDI once the regulations have been issued. As Canada finds its way as a middle power, its long-term interests will be best served by a strategy that recognizes China-US geopolitical uncertainty, shifting power relationships, and China's growing global prominence and assertiveness. Bilateral liberalization of trade and investment are key priorities, but the Huawei saga illustrates how national security has increased significantly in importance in this age of cyber security and digitalization. Multilateral pressures on China to adopt laws consistent with global standards are likely to be more effective than resorting to bilateral pressures to address differences in values and institutions. As long as Beijing refuses to engage in diplomatic exchange, its antagonism towards Canada in 2019 will prove difficult to manage in any but a step-by-step manner. Canada should also rely on international coalitions to press for normalization. All of these strategic elements will take time to develop and follow through; as other middle power partners have found, living with China requires focus, patience, and determination.

Acknowledgments

This book has several roots, the first planted more than forty years by a Canadian mentor who encouraged me as a newly minted PhD graduate from Princeton University to visit China to study the four modernizations and China's future. A visit a decade later focused on the early stages of the transformation of Shenzhen and Pudong from rice paddies to the expanding global industrial and technology centres we know today. A series of academic and policy links in Beijing, Shanghai, and other centres were other roots planted in the past century.

Throughout these years, China was an object of friendly curiosity to most Canadians and proved to be an attractive market with complementary trade. China sought secure supplies of food and natural resources Canada produces in abundance, while Canada sought security of demand from Chinese customers. Canada's relationships with China and the United States, as its overwhelmingly important trading partner and guarantor of its security, were managed separately. All of this began to change, however, as China grew to become the world's second-largest economy, as the United States objected to unfair Chinese trade and investment practices, and as the US-China relationship deteriorated towards a mutually damaging cold war with a US strategy of containment and Chinese determination to fight back.

The central focus of this book, however, is Canada's changing relationship with China, while recognizing that the US-China relationship is central to Canadians' collective future. For Canada and other middle powers located in proximity to one or both of these great powers, strategic choices are required. The economies of Australia, New Zealand, members of the Association of Southeast Asian Nations, and South Korea have realized significant economic benefits from their proximity to China while hedging their security with strong relationships with the United States.

The challenge is to learn to live with China. At present Canada lacks a China strategy, and so is vulnerable to pressures generated by the US-China relationship that might not best serve Canada's long-term interests. An example of such pressures is the current US administration's push to ban Chinese telecommunications giant Huawei's 5G technology from national mobile networks. The resulting political crisis has plunged our China relationship into a deep freeze and shone a spotlight on Canada's strategic priority, which is to shed our collective ignorance about China and learn to live with it as it really is.

Many people and organizations have been helpful in writing this book. Ongoing and timely exchange and collaboration with University of British Columbia colleague Paul Evans have been particularly valuable. Former ambassador David Mulroney has also contributed a thoughtful and realistic approach to learning about and living with China. At the University of Toronto Press, Jennifer DiDomenico has been consistently encouraging. A number of colleagues at the Rotman School of Management have been partners in various capacities. Vice Dean Ken Corts and Hai Lu, Professor of Accounting, have been significant partners in developing the China Initiative at the Rotman School. Critical inputs and perspectives have come from colleagues Bernardo Blum, Loren Brandt, Daniel Trefler, and participants from around the university and beyond in the quarterly China Research Workshops. Walid Hejazi played diverse roles as a colleague and in executing two Canada-China Business Surveys that provided insightful information on the business dimension of the bilateral relationship. Special thanks go to Sarah Kutulakos, executive director of the Canada China Business Council.

Colleagues in my international networks have also been valuable collaborators and critics. They include Peter Petri at Brandeis University, Shiro Armstrong at Australian National University, David Atnip at Gold Sands in Shanghai, Mary Boyd in Shanghai, and members of the sixteen-country Pacific Trade and Development network, whose International Steering Committee I chaired between 2013 and 2018. Participation in the International Finance Forum in Beijing and in Harvard University's Asia Vision 21 conferences, the Asia Global Institute in Hong Kong, and Ditchley Park seminars in England have also been useful sources of information and collaboration. Colleagues at Peking University's National School of Development and at the Peterson Institute for International Economics in Washington, DC, also engaged with me on intellectual and political questions. Participants in the Ottawa-based Public Policy Forum's 2018 project focused on a China strategy for Canada in 2018 offered timely Canadian perspectives. Thanks also go to three anonymous reviewers who provided critical and insightful comments.

Finally, very special thanks to Barry Norris, the talented editor of this and previous volumes. Despite an unfortunate arm fracture on my part just as final editing began, support from Barry and from Danica Chin and Audrey Lake made it possible to keep the book on schedule for timely publication.

NOTES

1. China's Rise

1 Modifying the list of superlatives in China's economic rise is a large gap in living standards within the country. By Asian Development Bank estimates, 5.7 per cent of Chinese still lived in poverty in 2015; see Asian Development Bank, *Asia 2050: Realizing the Asian Century* (Manila: ADB, 2011). The World Bank estimates that 4.1 per cent of the population lived below the international poverty line in 2014. A significant gap remains between current individual living standards in China – the World Bank ranks it in the "high middle-income" group – and those of high-income nations. Since 1978 closing that gap has been a priority, addressed by opening up and reforming the institutions and policies of China's previously planned and closed economy.

2 See William H. Overholt, "The West is getting China wrong," *East Asia Forum*, 11 August 2018.

3 "China inaugurates National Supervisory Commission," *Xinhua*, 23 March 2018, available online at http://www.chinadaily.com.cn/a/201803/23/WS5ab4d311a3105cdcf6513ed0.html.

4 "Xi calls for solid efforts to win Three Battles," *Xinhua*, 4 March 2018, available online at http://www.xinhuanet.com/english/2018-04/02/c_137083515.htm.

5 Kevin Rudd, "Xi Jinping's Vision for Global Governance," *Project Syndicate*, 11 July 2018, available online at https://www.project-syndicate.org/commentary/xi-jinping-has-a-coherent-global-vision-by-kevin-rudd-2018-07.

6 Xi Jinping, "Openness for Greater Prosperity, Innovation for a Better Future" (speech, 10 April 2018), available at http://www.chinadaily.com.cn/a/201804/10/WS5acc515ca3105cdcf6517425_1.html.

7 See Paul Heer, "Understanding the Challenge from China," Asan Forum, 3 April 2018, available online at http://www.theasanforum.org/ understanding-the-challenge-from-china/; and Michael D. Swaine, "The US Can't Afford to Demonize China," *Foreign Policy*, 29 June 2018, available online at https://foreignpolicy.com/2018/06/29/ the-u-s-cant-afford-to-demonize-china/.

8 Asia Society, Task Force on US-China Policy, *Course Correction: Toward an Effective and Sustainable China Policy*, February 2019, available online at https://asiasociety.org/center-us-china-relations/course-correction-toward-effective-and-sustainable-china-policy.

9 Reported by Xinhua, available online at http://news.xinhuanet.com/ enlish/photo/2015-11/04/c_134783513.htm, accessed 13 October 2016.

10 Lucy Hornby, "Communist Party asserts control over China Inc.," *Financial Times*, 3 October 2017. Note, however, that the provisions in the foreign investment law summarized in the previous chapter and due to take effect in January 2020 prohibit "illegal government interference" in joint ventures.

11 Zhang Zhong Xiang, "Powering a low-carbon China," *East Asia Forum*, 4 January 2017.

12 World Bank, Commission on Growth and Development, *The Growth Report: Strategies for Sustained Growth and Inclusive Development* (Washington, DC: World Bank, 2008), 19–21.

13 See, for example, Huang Yiping, "Can China Rise to High Income?" in *Asia and the Middle-Income Trap*, ed. Francis E. Hutchinson and Sanchita Basu (Abingdon, UK; New York: Routledge, 2016), 81–100.

14 See Bank for International Settlements, "Total Credit to the Non-financial Sector (Core Debt)," available online at https://stats.bis.org/statx/srs/ table/f1.1.

15 Tom Mitchell, "China's Xi orders debt crackdown for state-owned groups," *Financial Times*, 16 July 2017.

16 "China's new financial oversight body vows to fend of risks," *Reuters*, 8 November 2017, available online at https://www.reuters.com/article/ us-china-economy-committee/chinas-new-financial-oversight-body-vows-to-fend-off-risks-idUSKBN1D81OS.

17 International Monetary Fund, "IMF Executive Board Concludes 2018 Article IV Consultation with the People's Republic of China," Press Release 18/310, Washington, DC, 25 July 2018.

18 Ibid.

19 Gabriel Wildau, "China Internet finance crackdown targets fly-by-night operators," *Financial Times*, 21 April 2016.

20 "China to better regulate Internet finance," *Xinhua*, 14 October 2016.

21 Maggie Zhang, "PBOC sets up new committee to oversee China's burgeoning fintech industry," *South China Morning Post*, 15 May 2017.

22 Don Weinland, "China to end the year as worst performing stock market," *Financial Times*, 31 December 2018.

23 Gabriel Wildau and Yizhen Jia, "Collapse of Chinese peer-to-peer lenders sparks investor flight," *Financial Times*, 22 July 2018.

24 Nicholas Lardy, *Markets over Mao: The Rise of Private Business in China* (Washington, DC: Peterson Institute for International Economics, 2014), 72.

25 See "China Inc.: Reinstatement," *Economist*, 22 July 2017, 55–7.

26 Huang Yiping's advice was reported in "China central bank advisor calls for zombie company cleanup," *Financial Times*, 12 July 2017,

27 See Barry Naughton, "The Chinese Economy 'New Normal': Structural and Systemic Change" (paper presented at the conference "China's New Normal and Korea's Growth Challenge," Honolulu, November 2016).

28 "China Inc.: Reinstatement."

29 Don Weinland, "Alibaba and Tencent among investors in China Unicom," *Financial Times*, 16 August 2016.

30 Gabriel Wildau and Yizhen Jia, "China state groups gobble up struggling private companies," Financial Times, 26 September 2018.

31 See International Monetary Fund, "China's Emerging SOE Reform Strategy," in *The People's Republic of China: Selected Issues*, IMF Country Report 16/271 (Washington, DC: IMF, 2016), 38–43, available online at https://www.imf.org/en/Publications/CR/Issues/2016/12/31/The-People-s-Republic-of-China-Selected-Issues-44182.

32 Naughton, "Chinese Economy."

33 Nicholas Lardy, *The State Strikes Back: The End of Economic Reform in China?* (Washington, DC: Peterson Institute for International Economics, 2019).

2. China as a Global Innovator?

1 5G refers to "fifth-generation" wireless technology, which underpins the industrial Internet and machine-to-machine communication and is much faster than its 4G predecessor.

2 See Bien Perez, "China's chance to lead global innovation may lie with 5G mobile technology development," *South China Morning Post*, 1 October 2017, available online at https://www.scmp.com/tech/enterprises/article/2113581/chinas-chance-lead-global-innovation-may-lie-5g-mobile-technology, accessed 20 May 2018.

3 Naughton, "Chinese Economy."

4 Edward S. Steinfeld and Troels Beltoft, "Innovation Lessons from China," *MIT Sloan Management Review* 55, no. 4 (2014): 49–55.

5 World Bank and Development Research Center of the State Council, People's Republic of China, *China 2030: Building a Modern, Creative, and Harmonious Society* (Washington, DC: World Bank, 2013), 18, 25.

6 Paul Mozur and John Markoff, "Is China outsmarting America in AI?" *New York Times*, 27 May 2017, available online at https://www.nytimes.com/2017/05/27/technology/china-us-ai-artificial-intelligence.html.

7 China's R&D spending is 2.07 per cent of GDP compared with the OECD average of 2.38 per cent; see OECD, "Gross Spending on R&D," available online at https://data.oecd.org/rd/gross-domestic-spending-on-r-d.htm, accessed 8 December 2017.

8 McKinsey Global Institute, *The China Effect on Global Innovation* (n.p.: McKinsey and Company, October 2015), available online at https://www.mckinsey.com/~/media/McKinsey/Featured%20Insights/Innovation/Gauging%20the%20strength%20of%20Chinese%20innovation/MGI%20China%20Effect_Full%20report_October_2015.ashx.

9 "China's Audacious and Inventive New Generation of Entrepreneurs," *Economist*, 23 September 2017.

10 Jonathan Woetzel, Jeongmin Seong, Kevin Wei Wang, James Manyika, Michael Chui, and Wendy Wong, "China's Digital Economy: A Leading Global Force," Discussion paper (n.p.: McKinsey & Company, August 2017), available online at https://www.mckinsey.com/~/media/McKinsey/Featured%20Insights/China/Chinas%20digital%20economy%20A%20leading%20global%20force/MGI-Chinas-digital-economy-A-leading-global-force.ashx.

11 McKinsey Global Institute, *China Effect on Global Innovation*, 6.

12 "China's Audacious and Inventive New Generation of Entrepreneurs."

13 "Chinese fintech's global future is arriving now," *Financial Times*, 21 May 2018.

14 Woetzel et al., "China's Digital Economy," 10.

15 Paul Mozur, "Beijing wants AI to be $150b industry by 2030," *New York Times*, 20 July 2017, available online at https://www.nytimes.com/2017/07/20/business/china-artificial-intelligence.html.

16 See "Baidu Develops 'Medical Brain' for Computer-aided Diagnostics," *China Intellectual Property Blog*, 30 November 2016, available online at https://en.blog.chinabrand.de/2016/11/30/baidu-develops-medical-brain-for-computer-aided-diagnostics/.

17 Woetzel et al., "China's Digital Economy," 12–13.

18 Thomas Gatley, "The Expanding Universe of Private Companies," *GavelkalDragonomics*, 5 October 2017, available online at https://research.gavekal.com/search-result-list?search=&fr=&to=&au%5B0%5D=18816&selectItemau%5B0%5D=18816&sort=date&items_per_page=100.

19 See Martin Chorzempa, "Opinion: A Run on Peer-to-Peer Platforms Shouldn't Be Possible. It's Now Happening in China," *Caixinglobal*, 24 August 2018, available online at https://www.caixinglobal.com/2018-08-24/opinion-a-run-on-peer-to-peer-platforms-shouldnt-be-possible-its-now-happening-in-china-101318522.html.

20 See Peter J. Williamson and Eden Yin, "Accelerated Innovation: The New Challenge from China," *MIT Sloan Management Review*, 23 April 2014; and Wang Feng, Peter J. Williamson, and Eden Yin, "Antecedents and Implications of Disruptive Innovation: Evidence from China," *Technovation* 39–40 (May–June 2015): 94–104.

21 McKinsey Global Institute, *China Effect on Global Innovation*, 8.

22 Scott Kennedy, "Made in China 2025," Center for Strategic and International Studies, 1 June 2015, available online at https://www.csis.org/analysis/made-in-china-2025.

23 McKinsey Global Institute, *China Effect on Global Innovation*.

24 Kennedy, "Made in China 2025"; and Lee Xin En, "Made in China 2025: A New Era for Chinese Manufacturing," CKGSB Knowledge, 2 September 2015, available online at knowledge.ckgsb.edu.cn/2015/09/02/technology/made-in-china-2025-a-new-era-for-chinese-manufacturing/.

25 See Adam Segal, "When China Rules the Web," *Foreign Affairs* 97, no. 5 (2018): 10–18.

26 "China to establish national demonstration areas for 'Made in China 2025'," *Xinhua*, 20 July 2017.

27 Kennedy, "Made in China 2025."

28 Jost Wübbeke, Mirjam Meissner, Max J. Zenglein, Jaqueline Ives, and Björn Conrad, *Made in China 2025: The Making of a High-Tech Superpower and Consequences for Industrial Countries*, MERICS Papers on China 2 (Berlin: Mercator Institute for China Studies, December 2016), available online at https://www.merics.org/sites/default/files/2017-09/MPOC_No.2_MadeinChina2025.pdf.

29 Naughton, "Chinese Economy," 2.

30 Dan Wang, "Ideas: Why China Can Succeed in Tech," *GavekalDragonomics*, 19 December 2018, available online at https://research.gavekal.com/search-result?search=&fr=&to=&au%5B%5D=29274&selectItemau%5B%5D=29274&items_per_page=.

31 Loren Brandt, Wang Luhang, and Zhang Yifan, "Productivity in Chinese Industry: 1998–2013" (manuscript, University of Toronto).

32 Nicholas Lardy, "Private Sector Development," in *China's 40 Years of Reform and Development: 1978–2018*, ed. Ross Garnaut, Ligang Song and Cai Fang (Canberra: ANU Press, 2018), 329–44.

33 Henry Paulson, *Dealing with China: An Insider Unmasks the New Economic Superpower* (New York: Hachette Book Group, 2015), 375.

34 Regina M. Abrami, William C. Kirby, and F. Warren McFarlan, "Why China Can't Innovate," *Harvard Business Review* 92, no. 3 (2014): 107–11.
35 Ibid., 108.
36 McKinsey Global Institute, *China Effect on Global Innovation.*
37 Ibid., 10.
38 Greg Levesque, "Here's How China Is Achieving Global Semiconductor Dominance," *National Interest*, 25 June 2018..
39 Ibid.; Abrami, Kirby, and McFarlan, "Why China Can't Innovate."
40 See "Number of University Graduates in China between 2007 and 2017," *Statista*, available online at https://www.statista.com/statistics/227272/number-of-university-graduates-in-china/, accessed 9 August 2017.
41 An official development strategy was released in July 2017 with the goal of becoming the world's AI leader by 2030; see "Code Red," *Economist*, 27 July 2017.
42 See Wübbeke et al., *Made in China 2025*, 32, for a list of their smart factories.
43 Commission on the Theft of American Intellectual Property, "Update to the IP Commission Report: The Theft of American Intellectual Property: Reassessments of the Challenge and United States Policy" (Washington, DC: National Bureau of Asian Research, February 2017).
44 Susan Decker, "China becomes one of the top 5 US patent recipients for the first time," *Bloomberg*, 9 January 2018, available online at https://www.bloomberg.com/news/articles/2018-01-09/china-enters-top-5-of-u-s-patent-recipients-for-the-first-time.
45 Nicholas Lardy, "China: Forced Technology Transfer and Theft?" Peterson Institute for International Economics, 20 April 2018.
46 Josef Stadler, "Why China's business innovation can survive the trade war," *Financial Times*, 9 November 2018.

3. Creating a Leading Financial System

1 It should be noted that such behaviour was not unique to China. In the wake of the global financial crisis, one of the major criticisms of the US regulatory system was that regulators' knowledge and attention seriously lagged financial innovation.
2 See IMF, *People's Republic of China*, IMF Country Report 17/247 (Washington, DC: IMF, 2017), 10, 19, available online at https://www.imf.org/~/media/Files/Publications/CR/2017/cr17247.ashx.
3 The other four include the US dollar, the yen, the euro, and the pound sterling.
4 Seigniorage refers to the profit accruing to government by issuing currency, the financial value of which is much higher than the cost of producing it.

5   Barry Eichengreen, "The Renminbi Goes Global: The Meaning of China's Money," *Foreign Affairs* 96, no. 2 (2017): 157–63; and Yu Yongding, "Backpedalling or a step forward in renminbi reform?" *East Asia Forum*, 18 July 2017.

6   Andrew Sheng and Ng Chow Soon, *Shadow Banking in China: An Opportunity for Financial Reform* (Chichester, UK: John Wiley & Sons, 2016), 16.

7   Tom Mitchell, "China tightens rules on asset management to rein in risky lending," *Financial Times*, 17 November 2017.

8   See "China has made progress in tackling financial risks," *Financial Times*, 16 June 2018.

9   Yizhen Tian and Gabriel Wildau, "Chinese banks launch standalone wealth management units," *Financial Times*, 23 December 2018.

10 IMF, "IMF Executive Board Concludes 2018 Article IV Consultation."

11 Morgan Stanley, "China's eCommerce Revolution," Morgan Stanley Blue Papers (New York: Morgan Stanley, 13 March 2015).

12 Arjun Kharpal, "Alibaba sets new Singles Day record with more than $30.8 billion in sales in 24 hours," *CNBC*, 4 December 2018, available online at https://www.cnbc.com/2018/11/11/alibaba-singles-day-2018-record-sales-on-largest-shopping-event-day.html, accessed 20 February 2019.

13 Gabriel Wildau, "China bond party attracts few takers," *Financial Times*, 20 April 2017.

14 "View: China's real credit risk lurks in shadow finance," *Financial Times*, 31 May 2017.

15 China Securities Regulatory Commission, *China Capital Markets Development Report 2008* (Beijing, 2008), 289–90, available online at http://www.csrc.gov.cn/pub/csrc_en/Informations/publication/200911/P020091103520222505841.pdf.

16 Nicholas Borst, "China's Bond Market: Larger, More Open and Riskier," *Blog Entries*, Federal Reserve Bank of San Francisco, 20 May 2016, available online at http://www.frbsf.org/banking/asia-program/staff/nicholas-borst/.

17 Nicholas Lardy, "A Blueprint for Rebalancing the Chinese Economy," Policy Brief PB13-02 (Washington, DC: Peterson Institute for International Economics, 2013), 15.

18 Andrew Sheng, "No Pain, No Gain," University of Hong Kong, Asia Global Institute, 22 January 2016, available online at https://www.asiaglobalinstitute.hku.hk/news-post/no-pain--no-gain.

19 Jonathan Anderson, 2016. "Avoiding the Japan Trap: China's Impending Minsky Moment," *China Economic Quarterly* (March 2016): 9–16.

20 "China's third party payments providers will sever direct ties to banks," *China Banking News*, 6 April 2018, available online at http://www.chinabankingnews.com/2018/04/16/chinas-third-party-payments-providers-severe-direct-ties-bank/.

21 See "Governor Yi Gang announced measures and timetable for further financial sector opening-up at Boao Forum for Asia," People's Bank of China, 11 April 2018, available online at http://www.pbc.gov.cn/english/130721/3517991/index.html.

22 For details on these measures, see Kevin Rudd, "US-China Relations in 2019" (speech to the Asia Society, 5 December 2018), available online at https://asiasociety.org/blog/asia/kevin-rudd-us-china-relations-what-happens-next. See also China International Capital Corporation, "CICC: PRC Stresses Financial Support to Private Economy to Observe Subsequent Progress," *Aastocks*, 12 November 2018, available online at http://www.aastocks.com/en/stocks/analysis/stock-aafn-content/00998/NOW.907318/all.

23 Lardy, *State Strikes Back*, e-book, loc 2534; and Elizabeth Economy, *The Third Revolution: Xi Jinping and the New Chinese State* (New York: Oxford University Press, 2018).

24 "The Chinese Economy: Package Deal," *Economist*, 16 March 2019.

4. China Invests Abroad

1 All FDI data are from United Nations Conference on Trade and Development, *World Investment Report 2018: Investment and New Industrial Policies* ([Geneva]: UNCTAD, 2018), annex 2, figure. 4, available online at http://unctad.org/en/PublicationsLibrary/wir2018_en.pdf.

2 Karl P. Sauvant and Michael D Nolan, "China's Outward Foreign Direct Investment and International Investment Law," *International Economic Law* 18, no. 4 (2015): 893–934.

3 See JP Morgan, "China's Increasing Outbound M&A: Key Drivers Behind the Trend," 2017, available online at https://www.jpmorgan.com/global/insights/chinas-key-drivers; and PwC, "PwC M&A 2016 Review and 2017 Outlook," January 2017, available online at https://www.pwccn.com/en/mergers-and-acquisitions/ma-press-briefing-jan2017.pdf.

4 As indicated in Table 4.1, these transactions are listed in chronological order, as reported in *China Daily*, 1 June 2017.

5 Don Weinland, "Chinese M&A boom faces regulatory checks," *Financial Times*, 29 December 2016.

6 See "China's Dalian Wanda 2015 revenue up 19 pct as diversification takes hold," *Reuters*, 11 January 2016, available online at https://www.reuters.com/article/wanda-group-results-idUSL3N14V1DU20160111.

7 Zhang Shu and Matthew Miller, "China cracks down on Dalian Wanda's overseas deals: Sources," *Reuters*, 17 July 2017.

8 See Prudence Ho, "How HNA drama turned tragic as buying spree went sour," *Bloomberg*, 5 July 2018, available online at https://www.bloomberg.

com/news/articles/2018-07-05/hna-drama-turns-tragic-after-buying-spree-turns-sour-quicktake.

9 "Who owns HNA, China's most aggressive dealmaker?" *Financial Times*, 2 June 2017.

10 Don Weinland, Arash Massoudi, and James Fontanella-Kahn, "HNA's buying spree surpasses $40 billion with CWT deal," *Financial Times*, 9 April 2017.

11 See "Lexmark announces completion of acquisition by Apex Technology and PAG Asia Capital," News Release, 29 November, 2016, available online at http://newsroom.lexmark.com/2016-11-29-Lexmark-announces-completion-of-acquisition-by-Apex-Technology-and-PAG-Asia-Capital.

12 These platforms include QQ Instant Messenger, WeChat/Weixin, QQ.com, QQ Games, Qzone, and Tenpay.

13 Laura He, "Tencent is first Asian company to top US$500 billion in value, joining Apple and Facebook," *South China Morning Post*, 21 November 2017.

14 Clair Jones, Javier Espinoza, and Tom Hancock, 2017. "Overseas Chinese acquisitions worth $75 billion cancelled last year," *Financial Times*, 5 February 2017.

15 Missing from the lists is the largest-ever acquisition to date – of Syngenta, a Swiss agricultural firm, by the SOE ChemChina for $43 billion, which closed in 2017.

16 See Baker McKenzie, *Rising Tension: Assessing China's FDI drop in Europe and North America* (New York: Rhodium Group, 2019).

17 See Thilo Hanemann, Adam Lysenko, and Cassie Gao, 2017. "Tectonic Shifts: Chinese Outbound M&A in 1H 2017," Rhodium Group, 27 June 2917, available online at http://rhg.com/notes/tectonic-shifts-chinese-outbound-ma-in-1h-2017.

18 A major source for the ensuing discussion in this section is Thilo Hanemann, Daniel A. Rosen, and Cassie Gao, 2018. "Two-way Street: 2018 Update US-China Direct Investment Trends," Rhodium Group, 10 April 2018, available online at http://rhg.com/notes/tectonic-shifts-chinese-outbound-ma-in-1h-2018.

19 Thilo Hanemann, Cassie Gao, and Adam Lysenko, "Net Negative: Chinese Investment in the United States in 2018," Rhodium Group, 13 January 2019, available online at https://rhg.com/research/Chinese-investment-in-the-US-2018-recap.

20 Tom Hancock, "Chinese investment into US biotech startups soars," *Financial Times*, 1 July 2018.

21 Ibid.

22 See Lardy, "China: Forced Technology Transfer and Theft?"

23 Sarah Kutulakos et al., *Canada China Business Survey 2016* ([Toronto]: Canada China Business Council, 25 April 2017), 4.
24 United Nations Conference on Trade and Development, *World Investment Report 2015: Reforming International Investment Governance* ([Geneva]: UNCTAD, 2015), annex table 2.
25 See Wendy Dobson, "China's State-owned Enterprises and Canada's FDI Policy," *SPP Papers* (University of Calgary, School of Public Policy) 7, no. 10 (March 2014).

5. The Belt and Road Initiative

 1 World Bank, "Belt and Road Initiative," *Brief*, 29 March 2018, available online at https://www.worldbank.org/enn/topic/regional-integration/brief/felt-and-road-initiative.
 2 See, for example, John Hurley, Scott Morris, and Gailyn Portelance, 2018. "Examining the Debt Implications of the Belt and Road Initiative from a Policy Perspective," CGD Policy Paper 121 (Washington, DC: Center for Global Development, March 2018).
 3 See Nadège Rolland, *China's Eurasian Century? Political and Strategic Implications of the Belt and Road Initiative* (Seattle: National Bureau of Asian Research, 2017), 108.
 4 "China encircles the world with One Belt, One Road strategy," *Financial Times*, 3 May 2017.
 5 Eswar Prasad, "Path to Influence," *Finance & Development* 54, no. 3 (2017): 22–5, available online at https://www.imf.org/external/pubs/ft/fandd/2017/09/prasad.htm.
 6 Hugh White, "China's Belt and Road Initiative to challenge US-led order," *East Asia Forum*, 8 May 2017.
 7 See "How to respond to China's Belt and Road Initiative," *East Asia Forum Weekly*, 15 May 2017.
 8 See European Bank for Reconstruction and Development, "Belt and Road Initiative" (London, n.d.), available online at https://www.ebrd.com/what-we-do/belt-and-road/overview.html.
 9 See "FT View: China needs to act as a responsible creditor," *Financial Times*, 29 April 2018.
10 "China encircles the world with One Belt, One Road strategy," *Financial Times*, 3 May 2017.
11 For details, see Asian Infrastructure Investment Bank, "Approved Projects" (Beijing: AIIB, 2019), available online at https://www.aiib.org/en/projects/approved/.

12 See "China economy: Belt and Road Initiative Quarterly: Q2 2018," *Economist Intelligence Unit*, 21 May 2018, available online at http://country.eiu. com/article.aspx?articleid=626742246&Country=China&topic=Economy.

13 See "China signs more trade deals with Belt and Road countries," *Xinhuanet*, 31 May 2018.

14 See Gabriel Wildau and Ma Nan, "China new 'Silk Road' investment falls in 2016," *Financial Times*, 10 May 2017.

15 Tom Miller, "The Belt and Road to Leadership," *China Economic Quarterly*, June 2017, 9–16.

16 Miles Johnson, "Why would Italy endorse China's Belt and Road Initiative?" *Financial Times*, 21 March 2019.

17 See James A. Millward, "Is China a colonial power?" *New York Times*, 4 May 2018.

18 Ibid.

19 Miller 2017.

20 Nadia Naviwala, "Pakistan's $100B deal with China: What does it amount to?" *Devex*, 24 August 2017, available online at https://www.devex.com/new/pakistan-s-100b-deal-with-china-what-does-it-amount-to-90872.

21 Kamran Haider and Faseeh Mangi, "IMF bailout looms for Pakistan as debt surge raises alarm," *Bloomberg*, 30 May 2018, available online at https://www.bloomberg.com/news/articles/2018-05-30/imf-bailout-looms-for-pakistan-as-debt-surge-raises-alarm .

22 For this update, see Adnan Aamir, "China's Belt and Road plans dismay Pakistan's poorest province," *Financial Times*, 14 June 2018.

23 "Where Will China's 'One Belt, One Road' Initiative Lead?" Knowledge@ Wharton, 22 March 2017, available online at https://knowledge.wharton. upenn.edu/article/can-chinas-one-belt-one-road-initiative-match-the-hype/.

24 Ibid.

25 Neelam Deo and Amit Bhandari, "The intensifying backlash against BRI," Gateway House, 31 May 2018, available online at https://www.gatewayhouse. in/bri-debt-backlash/.

26 James Crabtree and Blake Berger, "Malaysia GE (general election) a wake-up call on China projects," *Straits Times*, 14 May 2018; see also Ben Bland, "Malaysian backlash tests China's Belt and Road ambitions," *Financial Times*, 24 June 2018; and Stefania Palma, "Malaysia resets China ties over 'lopsided' deals," *Financial Times*, 10 July 2018.

27 Millward, "Is China a colonial power?"

28 "China's Belt and Road Initiative is falling short," *Financial Times*, 29 July 2018.

29 Hurley, Morris, and Portelance, "Examining the Debt Implications."

30 "China needs to act as a responsible creditor," *Financial Times*, 29 April 2018.

31 Linda Lim, "The BRI needs fewer Chinese characteristics," *East Asia Forum*, 9 May 2018.

32 See, for example, Andrew M. Warner, "Public Investment as an Engine of Growth," IMF Working Paper WP14/148 (Washington, DC: International Monetary Fund, 2014), available online at https://www.imf.org/external/pubs/ft/wp/2014/wp14148.pdf.

33 James Kynge, Lucy Hornby, and Don Weinland, "China development banks expand links with foreign lenders," *Financial Times*, 15 July 2018.

34 David Lubin, "China's Belt and Road at 5: One-to-many or many-to-many?" *Financial Times*, 19 October 2018.

35 The Paris Club is an informal group of official creditors whose role is to find and coordinate sustainable solutions to payments difficulties of debtor countries. See http://www.clubdeparis.org.

36 See Agatha Kratz, "China in the Asia-Pacific: High-speed Rail Blues," *China Economic Quarterly*, June 2017.

37 See, for example, Lim, "BRI needs fewer Chinese characteristics"; and Alvin A. Camba and Kuek Jia Yao, "China's Belt and Road Initiative paved with risk and red herrings," *East Asia Forum*, 26 June 2018.

38 For this kind of argument, see Millward, "Is China a colonial power?"; and "Briefing: China's Belt and Road Initiative," *Economist*, 28 July 2018, 13–16.

39 Brenda Goh and Michael Martina, "China to recalibrate Belt and Road, defend scheme against criticism," *Reuters*, 23 April 2019, available online at https://www.reuters.com/article/us-china-silkroad-forum/china-to-recalibrate-belt-and-road-defend-scheme-against-criticism-idUSKCN1S00AZ.

40 Xi Jinping, keynote speech at the Belt and Road Forum for International Cooperation 2019, Beijing, 28 April 2019, available online at http://www.cpecinfo.com/news/the-complete-text-of-president-xi-jinping-speech-at-the-belt-and-road-forum-for-international-cooperation-2019/NzAwMQ.

6. Living with China

1 The other signatories must be informed in advance about the intent to enter into such negotiations and to share any draft agreement with them before signing. If other signatories object to the proposed agreement, they may terminate the USMCA with six months' notice – possibly replacing it with a bilateral agreement between the two remaining signatories. Initially this was seen as an infringement of Canada's sovereignty, but it was pointed

out that such information would normally be shared by trading partners as a courtesy, and in this case the United States has also bound itself.

2 These insightful perspectives are captured by Harvard professor Graham Allison in *Destined for War: Can America and China Escape Thucydides's Trap?* (Boston: Houghton Mifflin Harcourt, 2017), chap. 7.

3 See Xi Jinping, "Openness for Greater Prosperity, Innovation for a Better Future" (address to 2018 Boao Forum for Asia, Hainan, 10 April 2018), available online at https://www.uscnpm.org/blog/2018/04/11/transcript-president-xi-addresses-2018-boao-forum-asia-hainan/.

4 Joshua P. Meltzer, "A Reformed China Is a Stronger China, and Such Is the US Dilemma," *East Asia Forum*, 10 January 2019.

5 Available at https://www.hudson.org/events/1610-vice-president-mike-pence-s-remarks-on-the-administration-s-policy-towards-china102018.

6 See United States, *National Security Strategy of the United States of America* (Washington, DC: White House, 2017), available online at https://www.whitehouse.gov/wp-content/uploads/2017/12/NSS-Final-12-18-2017-0905.pdf.

7 See Paul Heer, "Understanding the Challenge from China," *Open Forum*, 3 April 2018; and Michael D. Swaine, "The US Can't Afford to Demonize China," *Foreign Policy*, 29 June 2018.

8 Allison, *Destined for War*, 221–30.

9 The Society for Worldwide Interbank Financial Telecommunication code (SWIFT) and the Internet Corporation for Assigned Names and Numbers (ICANN), a non-profit organization responsible for ensuring secure networks and stable operation.

10 David Mulroney, "Canada must see China for what it truly is," *Globe and Mail*, 29 December 2018.

11 Paul Evans and Xiaojun Li, "February 2019 Survey of Canadian Attitudes on China and Canada-China Relations" (Vancouver, University of British Columbia, School of Public Policy and Global Affairs, 7 March 2019).

12 The discussion in this and the ensuing section draws upon Wendy Dobson and Paul Evans, "The Future of Canada's Relationship with China," IRPP Policy Horizons Essay (Montreal: Institute for Research on Public Policy, November 2015), available online at https://irpp.org/wp-content/uploads/2015/11/policy-horizons-2015-11-17.pdf.

13 See Canada, "Public Consultations on a Possible Canada-China FTA" (Ottawa: Government of Canada, 8 November 2017), available online at https://international.gc.ca/trade-commerce/consultations/china-chine/report-rapport.aspx?lang=eng.

14 Study Group on Global Education, *Global Education for Canadians: Equipping Young Canadians to Succeed at Home and Abroad* (Ottawa: University of Ottawa,

Centre for International Policy Studies; Toronto: University of Toronto, Munk School of Global Affairs, November 2017), available online at http://goglobalcanada.ca/.

15 See Robert Fife and Steven Chase, "Ottawa launches probe of cyber security," *Globe and Mail*, 19 September 2018.

16 Janyce McGregor, "Banning Huawei from Canada's 5G networks could be costly for taxpayers," *CBC News*, 17 February 2019, available online at https://www.cbc.ca/news/politics/huawei-canada-china-fipa-1.5021033.

17 Ivy Li, "Huawei, a Risk that Canadians Cannot Afford," *Inside Policy* (Macdonald-Laurier Institute), March 2019, 25–6.

18 Robert Fife and Steven Chase, "No need to ban Huawei, Ottawa says," *Globe and Mail*, 24 September 2018.

19 Kishore Mahbubani, "The US strategy is not the best way to deal with Huawei," *Financial Times*, 6 March 2019 and Geoff Mulgan, "Build a global body to oversee telecom infrastructure," *Financial Times*, 5 May 2019.

20 Dobson and Evans, "Future of Canada's Relationship with China."

21 Trade with EU members collectively is larger.

22 See Canada, Global Affairs Canada, *Canada-China Economic Complementarities Study* (Ottawa: Global Affairs Canada, 2012), available online at https://www.international.gc.ca/trade-agreements-accords-commerciaux/agr-acc/china-chine/study-comp-etude.aspx?lang=eng.

23 Ensuing discussion of this list draws from Dobson and Evans, "Future of Canada's Relationship with China."

24 See Dobson, "China's State-owned Enterprises and Canada's FDI Policy"; and Dobson and Evans, "Future of Canada's Relationship with China."

25 For the text of the Joint Statement, see https://pm.gc.ca/eng/news/2016/09/23/joint-statement-between-canada-and-peoples-republic-china.

26 Kerry Sun, "China-Australia Free Trade Agreement: Implications for Canada," *University of Alberta, China Institute Occasional Paper Series* 2, no. 1 (2015), available online at https://cloudfront.ualberta.ca/-/media/china/media-gallery/research/occasional-papers/chaftakerrysun201503.pdf.

27 Ibid.

28 Laura Dawson and Dan Ciuriak, "Chasing China: Why an Economic Agreement with China Is Necessary for Canada's Continued Prosperity" (n.p.: Dawson Strategic and Ciuriak Consulting, 2016).

29 More sophisticated than the China-Australia agreement, this option would draw on features of both the TPP and CETA in the comprehensive negotiations. See Patrick Leblond, "Toward a Free Trade Agreement with China: Opportunities, Challenges and Building Blocks" (Waterloo, ON: Centre for International Governance Innovation, 2017), available online at https://www.cigionline.org/person/patrick-leblond.

30 The seven sectors identified in the 2012 study are agriculture and agri-food; clean tech and environmental goods; machinery and equipment in agriculture and mining; natural resources and related products, including pulp and paper; services; textiles and related products; and transportation.

31 See Public Policy Forum, *Diversification not Dependence: A Made-in-Canada China Strategy* (Ottawa, 2018), available online at https://www.ppforum.ca/publications/diversification-not-dependence-a-made-in-canada-china-strategy/.

32 The sectoral arguments presented here are based in part on the 2012 *Complementarities Study* and on an unpublished analytical background paper that I contributed to the Public Policy Forum as a participant in the process leading to the final report, written by Edward Greenspon and Kevin Lynch.

33 Many of these suggestions are made by the Asia Pacific Foundation of Canada in "Toward a Canada-China FTA" (Vancouver: Asia Pacific Foundation of Canada, 2017), available online at https://www.asiapacific.ca/sites/default/files/filefield/canada-china_fta_report_final_1.pdf.

34 Canada China Business Council, "Canada-China Business Survey 2018/2019: Summary," May 2019.

35 Nathaniel Vanderklippe, "Chinese visitor visa applications to Canada increase despite Huawei dispute," *Globe and Mail*, 23 February 2019.

36 Marie-Danielle Smith, "Canadian companies start to benefit from membership in China-based infrastructure bank," *National Post*, 25 March 2019.

37 Evan A. Feigenbaum, "Reluctant Stakeholder: Why China's Highly Strategic Brand of Revisionism is More Challenging than Washington Thinks," Carnegie Endowment for International Peace, 27 April 2018, available online at https://carnegieendowment.org/2018/04/27/reluctant-stakeholder-why-china-s-highly-strategic-brand-of-revisionism-is-more-challenging-than-washington-thinks-pub-76213.

38 The United Front of the Chinese Communist Party is part of the Party structure that works to reach out to, represent, and guide key individuals and groups in China and abroad; see, for example, Kuo, Mercy M. Kuo, "China's United Front Work: Propaganda as Policy," *Diplomat*, 14 February 2018, available online at https://thediplomat.com/2018/02/chinas-united-front-work-propaganda-as-policy.

39 For an account of CPC influence on public discourse in Canada, see Jonathan Manthorpe, *Claws of the Panda: Beijing's Campaign of Influence and Intimidation in Canada* (Toronto: Cormorant Books, 2019).

40 Damian Cave and Jacqueline Williams, "Australian law targets foreign interference. China is not pleased," *New York Times*, 28 June 2018, available online at https://www.nytimes.com/2018/06/28/world/australia/australia-security-laws-foreign-interference.html.

41 See "Australia's decision to ban billionaire seen as pushback against Chinese foreign influence," *CNA International Edition*, 7 February 2019, available online at https://www.channelnewsasia.com/news/world/australia-ban-billionaire-pushback-chinese-influence-politics-11209068.

42 For a summary, see, for example, "China and the West; at the Sharp End," *Economist*, 16 December 2017, 20–2.

43 David Mulroney, "With another life at stake, Ottawa's misguided vision of Beijing demands a reboot," *Globe and Mail*, 1 May 2019.

INDEX

Page numbers in bold refer to figures and tables